Soups

GENERAL EDITOR
CHUCK WILLIAMS

RECIPES
NORMAN KOLPAS

PHOTOGRAPHY
ALLAN ROSENBERG

TIME
LIFE
BOOKS

Time-Life Books
is a division of TIME LIFE INC.,
a wholly owned subsidiary of
THE TIME INC. BOOK COMPANY

President: John M. Fahey

TIME-LIFE BOOKS
President: John Hall
Vice President and Publisher, Custom Publishing:
 Susan J. Maruyama
Director of Custom Publishing: Frances C. Mangan
Director of Marketing: Nancy K. Jones

WILLIAMS-SONOMA
Founder/Vice-Chairman: Chuck Williams

WELDON OWEN INC.
President: John Owen
Publisher: Wendely Harvey
Managing Editor: Laurie Wertz
Consulting Editor: Norman Kolpas
Copy Editor: Sharon Silva
Editorial Assistant: Janique Poncelet
Design: John Bull, The Book Design Company
Production: Stephanie Sherman, Mick Bagnato
Food Photographer: Allan Rosenberg
Associate Food Photographer: Allen V. Lott
Primary Food & Prop Stylist: Sandra Griswold
Food Stylist: Heidi Gintner
Assistant Food Stylist: Danielle Di Salvo
Prop Assistant: Karen Nicks
Glossary Illustrations: Alice Harth

The Williams-Sonoma Kitchen Library
conceived and produced by Weldon Owen Inc.
814 Montgomery St., San Francisco, CA 94133

In collaboration with Williams-Sonoma
100 North Point, San Francisco, CA 94133

Production by Mandarin Offset, Hong Kong
Printed in China

A Note on Weights and Measures:
All recipes include customary U.S., U.K. and
metric measurements. Conversions are based on
a standard developed for these books and have
been rounded off. Actual weights may vary.

A Weldon Owen Production

Copyright © 1993 Weldon Owen Inc.
All rights reserved, including the right of
reproduction in whole or in part in any form.

Library of Congress
Cataloging-in-Publication Data:

Kolpas, Norman.
 Soups / general editor, Chuck Williams ;
recipes, Norman Kolpas ; photography,
Allan Rosenberg.
  p.   cm. — (Williams-Sonoma
  kitchen library)
 Includes index.
 ISBN 0-7835-0250-8 (trade) ;
 ISBN 0-7835-0251-6 (library)
 1. Soups I. Williams, Chuck.
II. Title. III. Series.
TX757.K65 1993
641.8'13—dc20   93-16086
                                              CIP

Contents

VEGETABLE & FRUIT SOUPS 15

POULTRY & MEAT SOUPS 59

SEAFOOD SOUPS 85

INTRODUCTION

"Soup's on!" With that simple phrase, home cooks have long summoned family and friends to the dining table.

Soup is synonymous with good eating, with satisfying nourishment. The reason is found in the humble nature of soup itself: the very essence of its ingredients is distilled into a flavorful, soothing concoction easily sipped from a spoon.

This book showcases soup in all its elemental simplicity and variety. It begins with an overview of the few pieces of equipment any kitchen should have for soup making, followed by instructions for preparing the most basic of soup ingredients: stocks of poultry, seafood, meat or vegetables, slowly simmered until they are rich enough to serve alone as a satisfying bowl of broth. There is even a recipe for making commercial broth taste fresh and full of flavor. The introductory section concludes with guidelines for puréeing soup, and for adding the final flourish—an attractive garnish.

The 45 recipes that round out the book are organized into three chapters: soups based on vegetables and fruits; soups made with meat and poultry; and soups featuring seafood. I hope you'll be inspired to make soup—whether one of these recipes or a soup of your own devising. In fact, I urge you to do so for dinner tonight or lunch tomorrow. Add some bread, a salad and perhaps a glass of wine, and in just a matter of moments you too can be ready to join legions of other cooks in that soul-stirring call: "Soup's on!"

Chuck Williams

EQUIPMENT

Basic cookware and kitchen tools assist in the preparation of a wide array of soups

The equipment shown here proves that few recipes could be simpler than soup. Not surprisingly, pots and pans predominate, from frying and sauté pans and small saucepans for precooking ingredients or simmering small quantities of soup to larger saucepans and stockpots for cooking soups in quantity or preparing your own stock.

A few specific tools will make soups easier to prepare. Sturdy wooden spoons, ladles and whisks, for example, stir and serve more efficiently. Well-made colanders and strainers and sieves remove solids from stocks and give soups more uniform consistencies. And a food processor or food mill easily purées soup to a smooth, thick texture.

1. Colander and Strainer Basket

For straining solids from stock or draining beans, pasta or other ingredients that are partially or totally cooked before being added to soups. Basket may also be used as a steamer insert in a stockpot when cooking shellfish for seafood soups.

2. Saucepan

For cooking simple soups that do not require larger-capacity pots.

3. Food Processor

For puréeing soups and chopping large quantities of ingredients. Especially when puréeing, use a standard- or large-capacity model fitted with the metal blade, and process soups in several batches to avoid splattering.

4. Ladles

For serving soups and for transferring them to a food mill or food processor for puréeing.

5. Wooden Spoon

For stirring soups and breaking up ingredients—especially canned tomatoes—while they simmer. Also useful for pressing purées through sieves.

6. Cutting Board

Choose one made of tough but resilient white acrylic, which is nonporous and cleans easily. Thoroughly clean the chopping surface after every use.

7. Frying Pan

Choose good-quality, heavy aluminum, stainless steel, cast iron or enameled steel for rapid browning of meats or other soup ingredients. Sloped, shallow sides facilitate turning and allow moisture to escape more easily for better browning.

8. Wire Whisks

For whisking liquids or enrichments into puréed soups, or for liquefying sour cream before it is added to soups.

9. Measuring Spoons

For measuring small quantities of ingredients such as herbs or salt. Select good-quality, calibrated metal spoons with deep bowls.

through its conical grinding disk, which also sieves out fibers, skins and seeds. Most models include both medium and fine disks for coarser or smoother purées.

14. Chef's Knife and Paring Knife
Larger all-purpose chef's knife for chopping and slicing large items or large quantities of ingredients. Smaller paring knife for peeling vegetables and cutting up small ingredients. Choose sturdy knives with sharp stainless-steel blades securely attached to sturdy handles that feel comfortable in the hand.

15. Vegetable Peeler
Curved, slotted swiveling blade thinly strips away vegetable peels. Choose a sturdy model that feels comfortable in your hand.

16. Cheesecloth
Used in double thickness to line strainers and filter out fine particles when straining a stock or a broth in which shellfish have been cooked. Muslin can also be used.

17. Skimmer
Wide bowl and fine mesh for efficient removal of froth and scum from surface of stock during its preparation.

18. Wire Strainer
For straining solids from soups that have been puréed in a food processor. Choose a sturdy stainless-steel model with a securely attached handle and wire mesh bowl, as well as a hook that will grip the lip of a mixing bowl.

10. Measuring Cups
For accurate measuring of dry ingredients. Choose a set in graduated sizes. For liquids use a heavy-duty, heat-resistant glass measuring cup.

11. Sauté Pan
For browning soup ingredients or for simmering. Select a well-made heavy metal pan. Straight sides, usually of about 2½ inches (6 cm), help contain splattering and permit simmering of small quantities of soup.

12. Stockpots
Tall, deep, large-capacity pots with close-fitting lids, for making stock, steaming shellfish or preparing large quantities of soup. Select good-quality heavy pots that absorb and transfer heat well. Anodized aluminum, shown here, or enameled steel cleans easily and does not react with the acidity of any wine, citrus juice or tomatoes.

13. Food Mill
Hand-cranked mill purées soups by forcing ingredients

STOCKS

The advantages of stocking up on a basic building block of rich and flavorful soups

Most soups rely upon stock—a rich essence of poultry, meat, fish or vegetables—for moistness and flavor. The stock you prepare at home will yield the finest-tasting soups of all. As the steps on the opposite page demonstrate, stock making is easy; and although time-consuming, it yields ample quantities, which can be refrigerated or frozen in small containers for future use.

Do not, however, be deterred from making soup if you don't have time to make stock. Seek out a good brand of canned broth at your local supermarket, or look for frozen or concentrated broth at specialty-food stores. If you like, give it an even fuller and fresher flavor by briefly simmering it with aromatic vegetables (see page 11).

Chinese Hot-and-Sour Soup with Duck

Chicken Stock

This is one of the most versatile stocks you can make. It is excellent served on its own, ladled over steamed rice or noodles. If you're not using all of it right away, freeze the unused stock in small containers. Stewing chicken parts make a particularly flavorful stock and are less costly than fryer or broiler parts.

1 leek, trimmed and carefully washed
6 lb (3 kg) stewing chicken parts
1 large yellow onion, unpeeled, root trimmed
1 large carrot, cut into 1-inch (2.5-cm) chunks
1 celery stalk with leaves, cut into 1-inch (2.5-cm) chunks
6 fresh parsley sprigs
3 fresh thyme sprigs
1 bay leaf
5 qt (5 l) water
½ teaspoon peppercorns
salt

Cut the white portion of the leek into 1-inch (2.5-cm) chunks and place in a large stockpot; reserve the green tops. Add the chicken, onion, carrot and celery to the pot. Sandwich the parsley, thyme and bay leaf between the reserved leek tops and securely tie with kitchen string. Add to the pot along with the water.

Over low to medium heat, slowly bring the liquid to a simmer, regularly skimming off the scum that rises to the surface until no more forms.

Add the peppercorns, cover partially and continue simmering gently for about 2 hours, skimming occasionally.

Line a strainer with a double layer of dampened cheesecloth (muslin) and set it inside a large bowl. Pour the contents of the pot into the strainer. Discard the solids. Season to taste with salt and let cool to room temperature; then refrigerate. A layer of fat will solidify on the surface of the stock; lift or spoon it off and discard. Stock may be stored in a tightly covered container in the refrigerator for up to several days or in the freezer for up to 6 months.

Makes about 4 qt (4 l)

BASIC STEPS FOR MAKING CHICKEN STOCK:

1. Making a bouquet garni.
To flavor the stock, make a bouquet garni by sandwiching parsley, thyme and a bay leaf between leek greens. Tie securely with kitchen string; add to the stockpot with chicken, vegetables and cold water.

2. Skimming the stock.
Over low to medium heat, bring the water to a simmer. Cover partially and simmer for about 2 hours. To help keep the stock clear and the flavor pure, regularly skim off scum as it rises to the surface, continuing until no more scum forms.

3. Straining the stock.
After the stock has simmered for about 2 hours, pour it through a strainer or colander lined with a double layer of dampened cheesecloth (muslin) set inside a large bowl. Reserve the chicken meat for another use; discard the other solids.

4. Skimming off the fat.
Season the stock to taste with salt and let it cool to room temperature. Cover and refrigerate. When it is thoroughly chilled, use a large spoon to remove the layer of fat solidified on its surface.

Fish Stock

Most fish markets will sell you heads, bones and trimmings for making stock. Use those from any mild white fish; avoid oily, strong-flavored fish such as mackerel, mullet, bluefish or salmon. If you like, add a few strips of lemon peel, a few white peppercorns, and some fresh fennel or dill sprigs to scent the stock gently. You can also replace half the water with dry white wine.

2 leeks, trimmed and carefully washed
4 lb (2 kg) fish heads (gills removed), bones and
  trimmings
2 yellow onions, sliced
2 carrots, sliced
2 celery stalks with leaves, sliced
6 fresh parsley sprigs
3 fresh thyme sprigs
1 bay leaf
4 qt (4 l) water
salt

Slice the white portion of the leeks and place in a large stockpot; reserve the green tops. Add the fish, onions, carrots and celery. Sandwich the parsley, thyme and bay leaf between the reserved leek tops and securely tie with kitchen string. Add to the pot along with the water.

Over low to medium heat, slowly bring the liquid to a simmer, regularly skimming off the scum that rises to the surface until no more forms. Cover partially and continue simmering gently for 30–40 minutes, skimming occasionally.

Line a strainer with a double layer of dampened cheesecloth (muslin) and set it inside a large bowl. Pour the contents of the pot into the strainer. Discard the solids. Season to taste with salt and let cool to room temperature. Cover tightly and refrigerate. Stock may be refrigerated for several days or frozen for up to 6 months.

Makes about 3 qt (3 l)

Meat Stock

A robust stock well-suited to meat or bean soups. Based on beef and chicken, it can also include veal bones; avoid using lamb or pork, unless you want a broth with their distinctive flavors. Store any stock you will not be using right away in small freezer containers.

2 leeks, trimmed and carefully washed
4 lb (2 kg) meaty beef bones such as shank (shin)
　　or short ribs
2 lb (1 kg) stewing chicken parts or wings,
　　backs or necks
6 cloves garlic, unpeeled
4 large carrots, cut into 1-inch (2.5-cm) chunks
2 celery stalks with leaves, cut into 1-inch (2.5-cm)
　　chunks
2 large yellow onions
3 whole cloves
6 fresh parsley sprigs
3 fresh thyme sprigs
1 bay leaf
5 qt (5 l) water
1 teaspoon peppercorns
salt

Cut the white portion of the leeks into 1-inch (2.5-cm) chunks and place in a large stockpot; reserve the green tops. Add the beef, chicken, garlic, carrots and celery. Stick the cloves into one of the onions and add both onions to the pot. Sandwich the parsley, thyme and bay leaf between the reserved leek tops and securely tie with kitchen string. Add to the pot along with the water.

Over low to medium heat, slowly bring the liquid to a simmer, regularly skimming off the scum that rises to the surface until no more forms. Add the peppercorns, cover partially and simmer gently for 3½–4 hours, skimming occasionally.

Line a strainer with a double layer of dampened cheesecloth (muslin) and set it inside a large bowl. Pour the contents of the pot into the strainer. Discard the solids. Season to taste with salt and let cool to room temperature, then refrigerate. A layer of fat will solidify on the surface of the stock; lift or spoon it off and discard. Stock may be stored in a tightly covered container in the refrigerator for up to several days or in the freezer for up to 6 months.

Makes about 4 qt (4 l)

*Sweet-and-Sour Cabbage
Soup with Flanken*

Vegetable Stock

Many of the soups in this book can become vegetarian dishes by using this flavorful vegetable stock instead of chicken or meat stock.

2 large leeks, trimmed and carefully washed
2 large carrots, sliced
2 large celery stalks, sliced
2 large yellow onions, sliced
3 cloves garlic, unpeeled
3 fresh parsley sprigs
2 fresh thyme sprigs
1 bay leaf
8 cups (64 fl oz/2 l) water
½ teaspoon white peppercorns
salt

Slice the white portion of the leeks and place in a large stockpot; reserve the green tops. Add the carrots, celery, onions and garlic to the pot. Sandwich the parsley, thyme and bay leaf between the reserved leek tops and securely tie with kitchen string. Add to the pot along with the water.

Over low to medium heat, slowly bring the liquid to a simmer, regularly skimming off the scum that rises to the surface until no more forms. Add the white peppercorns and continue simmering, partially covered, for 1–1½ hours.

Line a strainer with a double layer of dampened cheesecloth (muslin) and set it inside a large bowl. Pour the contents of the pot into the strainer. Discard the solids. Season the stock to taste with salt and let cool to room temperature. Cover tightly and refrigerate. Stock may be refrigerated for up to several days or frozen for up to 6 months.

Makes about 6 cups (48 fl oz/1.5 l)

Quick Full-Bodied Stock

Just 30 minutes or so of simmering with aromatic vegetables will help canned chicken or beef broth taste almost like homemade. Store any extra in the refrigerator for up to several days or in the freezer for up to 6 months.

3–4 cups (750 ml–1 l) canned broth
1 carrot, sliced
1 celery stalk, sliced
1 yellow onion, sliced
1 leek, white portion only, trimmed, carefully washed and sliced
1 bay leaf

Put all the ingredients in a saucepan and bring to a boil over low to medium heat, regularly skimming off the scum that rises to the surface until no more forms. Cover with the lid ajar and simmer for about 30 minutes.

Line a strainer with a double layer of dampened cheesecloth (muslin) and set it inside a large bowl. Pour the contents of the pot into the strainer. Discard the solids. The stock may be used immediately.

Makes 3–4 cups (24–32 fl oz/750 ml–1 l)

Puréeing

Using a food mill or food processor to give soup a smooth consistency and robust body

Many ingredients provide a soup with sufficient body to be puréed: root vegetables such as potatoes or carrots; tomatoes; bread crumbs; or cooked grains such as rice or sweet corn.

Puréeing is easily accomplished with either of two convenient tools. A hand-cranked food mill purées by forcing ingredients through its disk, which functions simultaneously as a sieve, removing fibers, skins and seeds from such vegetables as asparagus, corn and tomatoes. Most models come with both medium and fine disks, offering a choice of coarser or smoother purées.

A food processor purées soups almost in an instant, although subsequent sieving may be necessary to remove fibers, skins and/or seeds. Take care to purée hot soups in small batches in a processor, to avoid splattering. If you don't have a food processor, an electric blender may be used instead.

Using a Food Mill:

1. Ladling in the soup.
Assemble the food mill following the manufacturer's instructions and set it securely atop a large bowl. Ladle in the solids and liquid of the cooked soup.

2. Turning the mill.
Steadying the mill with one hand, turn its handle clockwise to force the ingredients through the disk. From time to time, turn the handle briefly counterclockwise to dislodge fibrous material from the disk's surface.

3. Finishing the purée.
Continue ladling the soup and turning the mill until all the ingredients have been puréed. Remove the mill and stir the purée to give it an even consistency, returning it to the pan if necessary for gentle reheating.

Using a Food Processor:

1. Puréeing the soup.
Insert the metal blade. Ladle in a small batch of the cooked solids and a bit of the liquid, taking care not to overfill the bowl. Close and pulse the machine several times, then process until the purée is the desired consistency.

2. Sieving the purée.
If there are fibers, skins or seeds you wish to remove—as in the tomato soup shown here—pour the purée into a sieve set over a large bowl.

3. Finishing the purée.
Using a large wooden spoon, press the purée through the sieve, discarding any solids trapped in the wire mesh. Repeat with the remaining purée in batches. Stir to give the purée an even consistency, returning it to the pan if necessary for gentle reheating.

GARNISHING

Easy, attractive ways to add a final, flavorful flourish to any bowl of soup

The simple act of adding a garnish to a bowl of soup just before serving can remarkably boost its appearance and flavor. As the six examples here show, all kinds of garnishes may be used: fresh herbs, shredded cheese, sour cream, croutons, or even a few reserved decorative pieces of the main ingredient.

Two or more compatible garnishes will make the soup look even more elegant. The only precaution is not to overwhelm the soup with too many garnishes. Subtlety always achieves the best results.

Puréed bell pepper
Roast, peel and seed a bell pepper (see glossary, page 106), then purée in a food processor fitted with the metal blade or in a blender. Spoon atop a rich, creamy soup, swirling it into a decorative pattern if you like.

Cheese
Scatter some shredded Cheddar, Swiss or other flavorful cheese—or freshly grated Parmesan—over a thick or robust soup.

Croutons
Cut slightly stale bread into slices ½–¾ inch (12 mm–2 cm) thick. Brush generously with olive oil, melted butter or a mixture of both. Cut into ½–¾-inch (12 mm–2 cm) cubes and spread on a baking sheet in a single layer. Bake in a 350°F (180°C) oven, turning occasionally, until crisp and golden brown, about 30 minutes. Scatter over a thick or robust soup. Croutons may be stored in an airtight container for 2–3 weeks; check for freshness before using.

Vegetable pieces
When making a puréed vegetable soup, reserve a few attractive pieces of the main ingredient— here, asparagus tips. Parboil in lightly salted water until tender-crisp and then float them atop the finished soup.

Sour cream
To enrich a soup, spoon in a dollop of sour cream, first whisking it in a mixing bowl to liquefy it slightly. Heavy (double) cream may also be used.

Fresh herbs
Cut fresh herbs— here, chives—into large or small pieces to scatter over soups of any kind.

Vegetarian White Bean Soup

1 cup (7 oz/220 g) dried small white
 (navy) beans
¼ cup (2 oz/60 g) unsalted butter or
 vegetable oil, or a mixture of both
1 large yellow onion, finely chopped
1 clove garlic, finely chopped
1 large carrot, finely chopped
1 celery stalk, finely chopped
5 cups (40 fl oz/1.25 l) vegetable stock
 (recipe on page 11)
1 can (1 lb/500 g) plum (Roma)
 tomatoes with their juice
1 teaspoon dried summer savory
1 teaspoon dried thyme
1 teaspoon sugar
1 bay leaf
salt and freshly ground pepper
2 tablespoons finely chopped fresh
 parsley

*It's surprising how much flavor vegetables alone bring to this
robust soup. Or, if you wish, you can add a large chunk of ham or
bacon, and make the soup with chicken or meat stock.*

Sort through the beans, discarding any impurities or
discolored beans. Put the beans in a bowl, add cold water to
cover and leave to soak for about 12 hours.

In a large saucepan, warm the butter and/or oil over
medium heat. Add the onion, garlic, carrot and celery and
sauté until the onion is translucent, 2–3 minutes. Drain the
beans and add them to the saucepan along with the stock,
tomatoes, savory, thyme, sugar and bay leaf. Bring to a
boil, reduce the heat to low, cover and simmer, stirring
occasionally to break up the tomatoes, until the beans are
very tender, 2–2½ hours. Discard the bay leaf.

Transfer about half of the soup to a food mill, a food
processor fitted with the metal blade or to a blender. Purée,
taking care to avoid splattering. Stir the purée back into the
pan, then season to taste with salt and pepper. Ladle into
warmed bowls and garnish with the parsley.

Serves 6–8

Carrot Soup with Caraway–Bread Crumb Topping

FOR THE CARROT PURÉE:

¼ cup (2 oz/60 g) unsalted butter

2 yellow onions, thinly sliced

2 lb (1 kg) carrots, thinly sliced

1 fresh tarragon sprig or 1 teaspoon
   dried tarragon

4 cups (32 fl oz/1 l) chicken stock or
   vegetable stock (recipes on pages 8–11)

⅓ cup (3 fl oz/80 ml) fresh orange juice

2 tablespoons fresh lemon juice

salt and white pepper

FOR THE TOPPING:

¼ cup (2 oz/60 g) unsalted butter

2 teaspoons caraway seeds

⅔ cup (1½ oz/45 g) fine fresh white
   bread crumbs

2 tablespoons finely chopped fresh
   parsley

Golden, buttered bread crumbs sautéed with caraway seeds provide a crisp, flavorful topping for the smooth, slightly sweet carrot purée. To ensure that the soup comes out at its best, choose slender, medium-sized carrots; avoid larger, woody carrots. Enrich the soup, if you like, with a splash of cream after sieving. The soup, minus the topping, is also good chilled.

❧

*F*or the carrot purée, melt the butter in a large saucepan over medium heat. Add the onions and sauté until translucent, 2–3 minutes. Add the carrots and tarragon, reduce the heat to low, cover and cook, stirring occasionally, about 10 minutes more. Add the stock and orange and lemon juices. Bring to a boil, reduce the heat to low, cover and simmer until the carrots are very tender, 10–15 minutes.

Discard the tarragon sprig, if using. In small batches, purée the soup in a food mill, a food processor fitted with the metal blade or in a blender, taking care to avoid splattering. Return the purée to the pan, season to taste with salt and white pepper and keep warm.

For the topping, melt the butter over low to medium heat in a frying pan. Add the caraway seeds and sauté for about 1 minute. Add the bread crumbs, raise the heat slightly and sauté, stirring, until golden brown, 2–3 minutes.

Ladle the soup into warmed bowls and scatter the bread crumbs generously on top. Garnish with the parsley.

Serves 6–8

Cream of Asparagus

¼ cup (2 oz/60 g) unsalted butter

1 mild onion, finely chopped

1 celery stalk with leaves, finely chopped

4 cups (32 fl oz/1 l) chicken stock or vegetable stock (*recipes on pages 8–11*)

3 lb (1.5 kg) asparagus, trimmed and cut into 1-inch (2.5-cm) pieces, tips reserved

2 baking potatoes, peeled and cut into 1-inch (2.5-cm) chunks

2 tablespoons finely chopped fresh basil or 1 teaspoon dried basil

2 cups (16 fl oz/500 ml) heavy (double) cream

salt and white pepper

Just a little onion, celery and basil are all that is needed to show off fresh asparagus in this luxurious, simple cream soup. It is also excellent served chilled, in which case be sure to add a little more salt and pepper to taste before serving.

In a large saucepan melt the butter over low to medium heat. Add the onion and celery and sauté until translucent, 2–3 minutes. Add the stock, all the asparagus stalks and about two-thirds of the tips, the potatoes and basil. Raise the heat and bring to a boil, skimming away any froth from the surface. Reduce the heat, cover and simmer gently until the vegetables are tender, about 20 minutes.

In small batches, purée the soup in a food mill. Or use a food processor fitted with the metal blade or a blender, taking care to avoid splattering. If you use a processor or blender, force the purée through a strainer with a wooden spoon to remove any fibers. Return the purée to the pan. Stir in the cream, season to taste with salt and white pepper, and warm over low heat.

Meanwhile, bring a small saucepan filled with water to a boil. Lightly salt the water and add the reserved asparagus tips. Cook just until tender-crisp, 3–4 minutes. Drain well.

Spoon the soup into warmed bowls and garnish with the asparagus tips.

Serves 6–8

Minestrone with White Beans and Pasta

½ cup (3½ oz/110 g) dried cannellini
  beans
2 tablespoons olive oil
1 yellow onion, finely chopped
1 clove garlic, finely chopped
5 cups (40 fl oz/1.25 l) meat stock,
  chicken stock or vegetable stock
  (recipes on pages 8–11)
1 can (1 lb/500 g) plum (Roma)
  tomatoes with their juice
1 large carrot, coarsely chopped
1 zucchini (courgette), coarsely chopped
¼ Savoy cabbage, outer leaves trimmed
  and discarded, cut into shreds
½ tablespoon dried basil
½ tablespoon dried oregano
½ tablespoon sugar
1 bay leaf
⅓ cup (2 oz/60 g) dried small elbow
  macaroni or shells
2 tablespoons balsamic vinegar
salt and freshly ground pepper
2 tablespoons coarsely chopped fresh
  parsley
⅔ cup (3 oz/90 g) freshly grated
  Parmesan cheese

Brimming with vegetables, pasta and beans, minestrone is Italy's best-known soup. Feel free to elaborate with whatever vegetables might strike your fancy. Diced potato can replace the pasta. Substitute kidney beans for the white beans, or use drained, canned beans instead of dried beans, adding them with the other vegetables. Coarsely chopped broccoli or cauliflower can stand in for the cabbage. Ham, pork or beef may also be added. Serve with crusty Italian bread.

Sort through the beans, discarding any impurities or discolored beans. Put the beans in a bowl, add cold water to cover and leave to soak for about 12 hours. Drain the beans and transfer to a heavy saucepan. Add water to cover by about 1 inch (2.5 cm) and bring to a boil over medium heat. Reduce the heat to low, cover partially and simmer very gently until the beans are tender and most of the liquid is absorbed, about 1½ hours.

When the beans have been cooking for about 1 hour, heat the oil in a large pot over medium heat. Add the onion and garlic and sauté until translucent, 2–3 minutes. Add the stock, tomatoes—coarsely breaking them up with a wooden spoon—carrot, zucchini, cabbage, basil, oregano, sugar and bay leaf. Cover partially and simmer until the vegetables are tender-crisp, about 20 minutes. Add the macaroni and cook, uncovered, until al dente, 8–10 minutes more.

Drain the beans and add to the pot along with the balsamic vinegar. Season to taste with salt and pepper. Ladle into warmed bowls. Garnish with the parsley and Parmesan.

Serves 6–8

Yankee Corn Chowder

2 tablespoons unsalted butter

1 yellow onion, coarsely chopped

1 large shallot, finely chopped

6 cups (48 fl oz/1.5 l) light (single) cream

8 ears corn, kernels removed with a sharp knife

salt and white pepper

2 tablespoons finely chopped fresh chives

1 red bell pepper (capsicum), roasted, peeled, seeded and puréed in a food processor or blender, optional

The freshest in-season corn is essential for this simple soup. For a smoky flavor, sauté some chopped bacon or ham with the onion and shallot. Swirled red pepper makes an attractive garnish.

❧

*I*n a large saucepan, melt the butter over low to medium heat. Add the onion and shallot and sauté until translucent, about 5 minutes. Add the cream and three-fourths of the corn kernels. Bring to a boil, reduce the heat and simmer, uncovered, until the corn is tender and the liquid thickens slightly, about 10 minutes.

In small batches, purée the soup in a food mill. Or use a food processor fitted with the metal blade or a blender, taking care to avoid splattering. If you use a processor or blender, force the purée through a strainer, pressing the solids with a wooden spoon. Return the purée to the saucepan over low to medium heat and add the remaining corn kernels. Simmer until the kernels are tender-crisp, about 5 minutes. Season to taste with salt and white pepper.

Ladle into warmed serving bowls, garnish with the chives and, if you like, spoon a swirl of puréed bell pepper atop each bowl (see page 13).

Serves 4–6

Split Pea Soup with Smoked Ham

Split peas seem made for the soup pot, cooking and softening in stock or water to produce a thick, satisfying bowlful. Use either yellow or green split peas. The soup is also good made with smoked turkey instead of ham.

2 cups (¾ lb/375 g) split peas
¼ cup (2 fl oz/60 ml) olive oil or
   unsalted butter
2 yellow onions, finely chopped
2 carrots, finely chopped
2 celery stalks, finely chopped
2 cloves garlic, finely chopped
6–8 cups (48–64 fl oz/1.5–2 l) chicken
   stock or water
1 piece smoked ham, ¾ lb (375 g)
2 large fresh parsley sprigs
2 bay leaves
1 teaspoon dried thyme
salt and freshly ground pepper
3 tablespoons finely chopped fresh
   parsley
lemon wedges

S ort through the peas, discarding any impurities or discolored peas. Set aside.

In a large pot, warm the oil or butter over medium heat. Add the onions, carrots, celery and garlic and sauté until the onions are translucent, about 5 minutes.

Add 6 cups (48 fl oz/1.5 l) of the stock or water, the peas, ham, parsley sprigs, bay leaves and thyme. Bring to a boil, then reduce the heat, cover and simmer gently, stirring occasionally, until the peas are reduced to a thick purée, about 1½ hours. Add more water or stock from time to time, if necessary, to keep the peas moist.

Before serving, discard the bay leaves and parsley sprigs. Remove the ham, chop it coarsely and stir it back into the soup. Season generously to taste with salt and pepper. Ladle into warmed soup bowls, garnish with the chopped parsley and serve with lemon wedges for guests to squeeze into individual portions.

Serves 6–8

Cream of Mushroom

2 lb (1 kg) fresh mushrooms
¼ cup (2 fl oz/60 ml) vegetable oil
¼ cup (2 oz/60 g) unsalted butter
4 large shallots, finely chopped
2 tablespoons all-purpose (plain) flour
5 cups (40 fl oz/1.25 l) heavy (double)
  cream
pinch of freshly grated nutmeg
salt and white pepper
2 tablespoons fresh lemon juice
1 tablespoon finely chopped fresh chives
1 tablespoon finely chopped fresh
  parsley

For a somewhat lighter soup, substitute 3 cups (24 fl oz/750 ml) chicken stock (recipe on page 8) for 2 cups (16 fl oz/500 ml) of the cream and increase the simmering time by 5–10 minutes to achieve the correct thick consistency. For a more flavorful version, stir in a generous splash of sweet or dry sherry, Madeira or white dessert wine just after you purée the soup.

Set aside 4 attractive mushrooms. Finely chop the remaining mushrooms.

In a large saucepan, warm the oil and butter over medium heat. Add the chopped mushrooms and shallots, raise the heat and sauté, stirring frequently, until the vegetables cook down to a thick, dark brown paste, 25–30 minutes. Part-way through the cooking time, when the mushrooms' liquid has evaporated, sprinkle in the flour and then stir it in.

Add the cream and deglaze the pan by stirring and scraping to dislodge any browned bits. Simmer, stirring occasionally, until thick, 15–20 minutes more.

In small batches, purée the soup in a food mill, a food processor fitted with the metal blade or in a blender, taking care to avoid splattering. Return to the pan and heat gently, stirring in the nutmeg and salt and white pepper to taste.

Meanwhile, cut the reserved mushrooms into neat slices about ¼ inch (6 mm) thick. In a small bowl, toss them with the lemon juice.

Ladle the soup into warmed bowls and garnish with the mushroom slices, chives and parsley.

Serves 4–6

Chilled Beet Borscht with Sour Cream and Vodka

6 cups (48 fl oz/1.5 l) meat stock or
vegetable stock (recipes on pages 10–11)
2 lb (1 kg) beets (beetroots), peeled and
coarsely shredded
1 bay leaf
½ cup (4 fl oz/125 ml) fresh orange juice
1 cucumber
2 green (spring) onions
2 cups (16 fl oz/500 ml) sour cream
⅓ cup (3 fl oz/80 ml) vodka, optional
salt and white pepper
2 tablespoons finely chopped fresh dill

Beet soups, served hot or cold, are popular throughout Eastern Europe. This simple version gains extra spark from the addition, just before serving, of a shot of vodka, which plays a role similar to that of the home-brewed kvas — a simple beer fermented from rye bread — or fermented beet juice traditionally added to the soup. Of course, you can leave the vodka out. Serve with sliced pumpernickel bread and butter.

In a large pot, combine the stock, beets and bay leaf and bring to a boil over medium heat. Reduce the heat to low, cover and simmer gently for about 30 minutes. Stir in the orange juice and let cool to room temperature. Discard the bay leaf, cover the soup and refrigerate until well chilled, 2–3 hours, or for up to 2–3 days.

Chill serving bowls in the refrigerator.

Peel the cucumber and cut in half lengthwise. Remove the seeds and discard. Dice the cucumber, place in a small bowl, cover and chill. Trim the green onions and slice thinly, including the tender green parts. Place in another small bowl, cover and chill.

Shortly before serving, remove the soup from the refrigerator and spoon off any solidified fat from its surface. Put 1½ cups (12 fl oz/375 ml) of the sour cream into a mixing bowl. Stir in the vodka and a ladleful of the chilled beet broth until thoroughly blended; then stir the sour cream mixture back into the soup. Season to taste with salt and white pepper.

Distribute the chilled cucumber and green onions evenly among the chilled bowls. Ladle in the soup and garnish with dollops of the remaining sour cream and a sprinkle of dill.

Serves 6–8

Spicy Seven-Bean Soup

¼ cup (1½ oz/45 g) each dried baby
lima beans, black-eyed peas, chick-
peas (garbanzo beans), kidney beans,
small white (navy) beans, pinto beans
and red beans
¼ cup (2 fl oz/60 ml) olive oil
2 cloves garlic, finely chopped
1 green or red bell pepper (capsicum),
seeded, deribbed and diced
1 large fresh green Anaheim chili pepper,
finely chopped
1 yellow onion, finely chopped
1 carrot, finely chopped
1 celery stalk, finely chopped
1 teaspoon red pepper flakes
4 cups (32 fl oz/1 l) chicken stock,
vegetable stock (recipes on pages 8–11)
or water
1 can (1 lb/500 g) crushed tomatoes
2 tablespoons tomato paste
1 tablespoon sugar
1 tablespoon dried basil
1 tablespoon dried oregano
1 tablespoon balsamic vinegar or red
wine vinegar
½ tablespoon dried thyme
2 bay leaves
salt and freshly ground pepper
½ cup (¾ oz/20 g) finely chopped fresh
parsley or cilantro (fresh coriander)

*This could just as easily be a three-, four-, five- or six-bean soup,
and could include beans other than those mentioned—just so long
as you start with the same volume of dried beans. The point is the
variety of subtly different colors, shapes and tastes that wind up in
the bowl. Leave out the chili pepper if you want a milder version.
Add some smoked ham or spicy sausage if you like, too.*

Sort through the beans, discarding any impurities or
discolored beans. Put the beans in a bowl, add cold water to
cover and leave to soak for about 12 hours.

In a large pot warm the oil over medium heat. Add the
garlic, bell pepper, chili pepper, onion, carrot, celery and
pepper flakes. Sauté until the onion is translucent, 2–3
minutes. Drain the beans and stir them into the pot along
with the stock, tomatoes, tomato paste, sugar, basil,
oregano, vinegar, thyme and bay leaves. Bring to a boil,
reduce the heat to low, cover partially and simmer until the
beans are tender, 2–2½ hours.

Just before serving, discard the bay leaves. Season to taste
with salt and pepper and stir in the parsley or cilantro. Ladle
into warmed bowls.

Serves 6–8

31

Cold Cherry Soup with Kirsch

2 lb (1 kg) ripe red cherries, pitted, with
   pits reserved

1 cup (8 fl oz/250 ml) water

1 cup (8 fl oz/250 ml) Riesling,
   Gewürztraminer or other medium-dry
   white wine

¼ cup (2 oz/60 g) sugar

¼ cup (2 fl oz/60 ml) fresh lemon juice

¼ cup (2 fl oz/60 ml) kirsch

1 tablespoon grated or shredded lemon
   zest, plus extra for garnish

2½ cups (20 fl oz/625 ml) sour cream

fresh mint sprigs

In high summer, when cherries are at their best, this simple soup, a traditional Hungarian specialty, makes a refreshing appetizer. You could even serve it for dessert! Leave out the kirsch, if you wish. And try substituting plain yogurt for the sour cream. If cherries aren't in season, the soup is fine made with frozen pitted cherries; just omit the first 5 minutes of simmering.

❧

In a large saucepan, combine the cherry pits, water, wine, sugar and lemon juice over medium heat. Bring to a boil, reduce the heat to low and simmer, uncovered, for about 5 minutes. Remove from the heat, cover and let steep for 5 minutes more. Pour the liquid through a strainer set inside a bowl; discard the pits.

Return the liquid to the pan. Add the pitted cherries, reserving about ⅓ cup (1½ oz/45 g) in a covered bowl in the refrigerator. Over medium heat, bring the liquid back to a boil; reduce the heat and simmer gently for 5 minutes more.

In small batches, purée the soup in a food mill, a food processor fitted with the metal blade or in a blender, taking care to avoid splattering. Transfer to a mixing bowl and stir in the kirsch and lemon zest. Let the soup cool to warm room temperature, then cover tightly and refrigerate until well chilled, 2–3 hours. Chill serving bowls.

Before serving, put 2 cups (16 fl oz/500 ml) of the sour cream in a tureen and whisk briskly to liquefy it slightly. Then gradually whisk in the soup. Ladle into the chilled bowls and garnish with dollops of the remaining sour cream, the reserved cherries, lemon zest and mint sprigs.

Serves 6–8

Cold Cream of Cucumber with Dill and Yogurt

6 pickling cucumbers, each about
   5 inches (13 cm) long, ends trimmed,
   unpeeled, cut into large chunks
3 or 4 sour dill pickles (pickled
   cucumbers)
2 cups (1 lb/500 g) plain low-fat yogurt
2 cups (16 fl oz/500 ml) heavy (double)
   cream
2 tablespoons fresh lemon juice
2 tablespoons finely chopped fresh dill
   or 1 tablespoon dried dill
salt and white pepper
fresh dill sprigs or dried dill for garnish

Inspired by two Indian dishes—the yogurt-and-vegetable salad known as raita *and the yogurt drink* lassi—*this refreshing soup is perfect for lunchtime on a hot summer day. A blender may be used for making this soup, but the ingredients may need to be mixed in batches, depending upon the blender capacity. Try adding finely shredded carrot or a little finely chopped sweet red (Spanish) onion to the mixture, or use them as garnishes. Fresh mint makes a good substitute for the dill. Serve with thinly sliced brown bread and butter.*

Put the cucumbers, pickles, yogurt, cream, lemon juice and chopped or dried dill in a food processor fitted with the metal blade and process until the vegetables are finely chopped. Season to taste with salt and white pepper.

Cover tightly and refrigerate until well chilled, 2–3 hours. Chill serving bowls.

Adjust the seasoning and ladle the soup into the chilled bowls. Garnish with dill sprigs or a sprinkle of dried dill.

Serves 6–8

35

French Onion Soup Gratinée

½ cup (4 oz/125 g) unsalted butter
4 large yellow onions, thinly sliced
salt
5 cups (40 fl oz/1.25 l) meat stock (recipe on page 10)
2 bay leaves
freshly ground pepper
½ lb (250 g) Gruyère or Swiss cheese, shredded
4–6 slices French bread, ½ inch (12 mm) thick and toasted golden brown

The secret to a good onion soup is to cook the onions very slowly, so their sugar content can caramelize. In old Paris bistros, this soup would be made with water—the deeply caramelized onions providing the only flavor and color. Good meat stock makes it taste even better. For a more complex flavor still, sauté some thinly sliced leek or shallot with the onions. You can also sprinkle on grated Parmesan before adding the Gruyère or Swiss cheese.

In a large saucepan, melt the butter over low heat. Add the onions and sprinkle to taste with salt. Stir to coat well with the butter, cover and cook, stirring occasionally, until very tender, 20–30 minutes.

Remove the cover, raise the heat slightly and sauté, stirring frequently, until the onions turn a deep caramel brown, about 1 hour; take care not to let them burn.

Add the stock and bay leaves, bring to a boil, reduce the heat, cover and simmer about 30 minutes more. Meanwhile, preheat a broiler (griller).

Discard the bay leaves. Taste the soup and adjust the seasoning with salt and pepper. Ladle the soup into heavy flameproof serving crocks or bowls placed on a baking sheet or broiler tray. Sprinkle a little of the cheese into each bowl, then place the toasted bread slices on top. Sprinkle evenly with the remaining cheese. Broil (grill) until the cheese is bubbly and golden, 2–3 minutes. Serve immediately.

Serves 4–6

Two-Mushroom Barley Soup

½ oz (15 g) dried porcini mushrooms

2 tablespoons vegetable oil

2 tablespoons unsalted butter

1 yellow onion, finely chopped

1 celery stalk, finely chopped

1 carrot, finely chopped

½ lb (250 g) fresh mushrooms, thinly sliced

2½ qt (2.5 l) beef stock or chicken stock (recipes on pages 8–10)

2 cups (¾ lb/375 g) pearl barley, rinsed under cold running water

1 bay leaf

salt and freshly ground pepper

4 tablespoons finely chopped fresh parsley

This thick, satisfying soup is enriched by the flavor of both fresh and dried mushrooms. Cook small chunks of beef or pork in it, if you wish, browning them in the oil before adding the vegetables. Or make a vegetarian version of the soup, using vegetable stock (recipe on page 11); the mushrooms taste meaty enough on their own. You can also enhance the soup with the addition of 1 can (1 lb/500 g) tomatoes with their juice, adding them with the barley. Serve with rye or sourdough bread.

Put the porcini mushrooms in a small bowl and add lukewarm water to cover. Soak until softened, about 30 minutes. Line a strainer with a double layer of cheesecloth (muslin) and set it inside a bowl. Pour the porcini and their liquid into the strainer, reserving the liquid. Finely chop the porcini and set aside.

In a large pot, warm the oil and butter over medium heat. Add the onion, celery and carrot and sauté until the onion is translucent, 2–3 minutes. Add the sliced fresh mushrooms, raise the heat and sauté until the mushrooms begin to soften, 2–3 minutes more.

Add the stock, barley, bay leaf and reserved porcini and soaking liquid and bring to a boil. Reduce the heat to low, cover partially and simmer gently, stirring occasionally, until the barley is tender and the soup is thick, 50–60 minutes.

Discard the bay leaf. Season to taste with salt and pepper. Ladle into warmed bowls and garnish with the parsley.

Serves 8–10

Pumpkin Soup with Gruyère

1 pumpkin, 5–6 lb (2.5–3 kg)

¼ cup (2 oz/60 g) unsalted butter

1 large yellow onion, finely chopped

6 cups (48 fl oz/1.5 l) chicken stock or vegetable stock (recipes on pages 8–11)

1 bay leaf

1½ cups (12 fl oz/375 ml) light (single) cream

2 tablespoons grated orange zest

2 tablespoons fresh orange juice

1 tablespoon fresh lemon juice

⅛ teaspoon freshly grated nutmeg

⅛ teaspoon ground ginger

¾ lb (375 g) Gruyère or Swiss cheese, shredded

salt and white pepper

2 tablespoons finely chopped fresh chives

The bright orange color of this soup surprises almost as much as its subtle flavor. You could serve the soup in one large pumpkin shell or small individual ones: Cut off the stem end of the pumpkin. Using a sharp-edged spoon or a melon baller, carefully scoop out the flesh, leaving a shell ½ inch (12 mm) thick. Fill the shell with the soup and scatter crisp croutons (see page 13) on top.

Cut the pumpkin in half and scoop out any strings and seeds. With a sturdy knife, cut away the hard peel. Coarsely chop the flesh; you should have about 8 cups (4 lb/2 kg). (If you would like to serve the soup in the pumpkin shell, see note above.)

In a large saucepan, melt the butter over medium heat. Add the onion and sauté until it begins to turn golden, 4–5 minutes. Add the stock, chopped pumpkin and bay leaf. Bring to a boil, reduce the heat, cover and simmer until tender, 15–30 minutes. Discard the bay leaf.

In small batches, purée the soup in a food mill, a food processor fitted with the metal blade or in a blender, taking care to avoid splattering. Return the purée to the pan and stir in the cream, orange zest, orange and lemon juices, nutmeg and ginger. Reserve a handful of the cheese and sprinkle the rest into the soup; stir over low heat until the cheese melts and blends in.

Season to taste with salt and white pepper. Pour into a warmed tureen or individual bowls and garnish with the reserved cheese and the chives.

Serves 10–12

Quick Vegetable Soup

2 tablespoons olive oil or unsalted butter

1 large yellow onion, coarsely chopped

1 cup (5 oz/155 g) coarsely chopped
   baking potato

1 cup (5 oz/155 g) coarsely chopped
   carrots

1 cup (4 oz/125 g) coarsely chopped
   broccoli

3 cups (24 fl oz/750 ml) chicken stock,
   meat stock or vegetable stock (recipes
   on pages 8–11)

1 teaspoon dried oregano

1 teaspoon dried thyme

1 bay leaf

salt and freshly ground pepper

You can make this quick soup with just about any combination of fresh vegetables on hand. Just be sure to include some potatoes or carrots. Leave the vegetables chunky for a robust soup, purée half of the vegetables for extra body, or purée the entire soup for a thick purée. For an extra-rich purée, stir in some cream or a chunk of butter just before serving.

❧

In a large saucepan, warm the oil or butter over medium heat. Add the onion and sauté until it begins to soften, 3–5 minutes. Add all the vegetables, the stock and herbs and bring to a boil. Reduce the heat and simmer until the vegetables are tender, 15–20 minutes.

Discard the bay leaf, season to taste with salt and pepper and serve. Or, if you like, purée part or all of the soup in small batches. Use a food mill, a food processor fitted with the metal blade or a blender, taking care to avoid splattering. Return the purée to the pan and heat gently to serving temperature. Adjust the seasoning and serve.

Serves 4–6

Cream of Broccoli with Aged Cheddar

1½ lb (750 g) broccoli, trimmed and tough stems peeled

2 tablespoons unsalted butter

1 yellow onion, finely chopped

¼ cup (1 oz/30 g) all-purpose (plain) flour

5 cups (40 fl oz/1.25 l) chicken stock or vegetable stock, heated (recipes on pages 8–11)

½ teaspoon dried thyme

1 tablespoon lemon juice

2 cups (16 fl oz/500 ml) milk

½ lb (250 g) aged sharp Cheddar cheese, shredded

salt and white pepper

Try cauliflower in place of the broccoli, and sauté some chopped bacon along with the onion if you like.

Reserve ½ cup (1 oz/30 g) small florets from the broccoli. Coarsely chop the remaining broccoli and set aside.

In a large saucepan, melt the butter over medium heat. Add the onion and sauté until it begins to brown, 5–7 minutes. Sprinkle in the flour and sauté, stirring, for about 1 minute more. Whisking continuously, slowly pour in the stock. Add the chopped broccoli, thyme and lemon juice and bring to a boil. Reduce the heat to low, cover and simmer until the broccoli is very tender, about 20 minutes.

About 5 minutes before the broccoli is done, bring a small saucepan filled with water to a boil and lightly salt the water. Add the reserved florets and simmer until tender-crisp, 3–5 minutes. Drain and keep warm.

In small batches, purée the soup in a food mill, a food processor fitted with the metal blade or in a blender, taking care to avoid splattering. Return the purée to the pan, stir in the milk and bring to a simmer over low heat.

Reserve a small handful of the cheese and sprinkle the rest into the soup; stir over low heat until the cheese melts and blends in. Season to taste with salt and white pepper. Ladle into warmed bowls and garnish with the cooked broccoli florets and reserved cheese.

Serves 6–8

Fresh Tomato Cream

¼ cup (2 oz/60 g) unsalted butter

1 red (Spanish) onion, finely chopped

1 small carrot, finely chopped

4 lb (2 kg) ripe tomatoes, peeled and coarsely chopped

3 cups (24 fl oz/750 ml) chicken stock or vegetable stock (*recipes on pages 8–11*)

1 fresh basil sprig

½ teaspoon dried thyme

1 bay leaf

1½ cups (4 oz/125 g) firmly packed fresh white bread crumbs

1 cup (8 fl oz/250 ml) light (single) cream

salt and white pepper

2 tablespoons finely shredded fresh basil leaves for garnish

Make this soup in high summer, when farmer's markets offer peak-of-season, deep red, vine-ripened tomatoes. If the tomatoes are less than at their best, add 1 tablespoon sugar to the soup. A little grated fresh ginger, grated orange zest or a splash of orange juice or sherry can also be added to enliven the soup. Serve with crackers or buttered toast.

*I*n a large saucepan, melt the butter over medium heat. Add the onion and carrot and sauté until the onion is translucent, 2–3 minutes. Add the tomatoes, stock, basil sprig, thyme and bay leaf. Bring to a boil, reduce the heat, cover and simmer for about 30 minutes.

Discard the bay leaf and stir in the bread crumbs. In small batches, purée the soup in a food mill. Or use a food processor fitted with the metal blade or a blender, taking care to avoid splattering. If you use a processor or blender, force the purée through a strainer using a wooden spoon. Return the purée to the pan, stir in the cream and warm thoroughly over low heat.

Season to taste with salt and white pepper. Ladle into warmed bowls and garnish with the shredded basil.

Serves 6–8

Hungarian Cauliflower Soup

8 cups (64 fl oz/2 l) milk
1 yellow onion, finely chopped
1 carrot, finely chopped
6 oz (185 g) cooked ham, cut into small
dice
1 head cauliflower
½ cup (4 fl oz/125 ml) sour cream
2 teaspoons salt
white pepper

Chuck Williams was served a delicious cauliflower soup on a visit to the famous Herend porcelain factory in Hungary. When he returned to San Francisco, he developed this recipe, which comes as close as possible to the original. If you like, lightly sprinkle individual servings with a dash of sweet Hungarian paprika.

In a saucepan bring the milk to a boil. Strain it through a fine strainer into a large pot. Add the onion, carrot and ham. Cover partially and simmer gently over medium heat for 10 minutes, taking care that it does not boil over.

Meanwhile, remove the florets from the cauliflower head and chop them coarsely. Measure out 4 cups (10 oz/315 g) and add to the soup. Simmer for 15 minutes more.

In a small bowl stir a little of the hot soup into the sour cream until smooth. Add this mixture to the remaining soup along with the salt and some white pepper to taste. Simmer briefly, stirring well. Adjust the seasoning and ladle into warmed bowls.

Serves 4–6

49

Gazpacho

1½ cups (3 oz/90 g) fresh sourdough or coarse country bread crumbs

½ cup (4 fl oz/125 ml) extra-virgin olive oil

2 cloves garlic

1 red (Spanish) onion, finely chopped

1 cucumber, peeled, cut in half lengthwise, seeded and finely chopped

1 green bell pepper (capsicum), seeded, deribbed and finely chopped

4 ripe tomatoes, peeled and coarsely chopped

2 cups (16 fl oz/500 ml) tomato juice, chilled

2 cups (16 fl oz/500 ml) water, chilled

¼ cup (2 fl oz/60 ml) red wine vinegar

salt and white pepper

1 cup (8 fl oz/250 ml) sour cream

1 cup (1½ oz/45 g) small croutons (see page 13)

2 eggs, hard cooked, whites and yolks separated and finely chopped

A specialty of the Andalusia region of southern Spain, this chilled soup tastes as fresh as a salad, highlighting ripe summertime vegetables—particularly tomatoes. A food processor speeds the preparation. (A blender may also be used, but you may need to prepare the soup in batches.) If good sun-ripened tomatoes are unavailable, substitute canned plum (Roma) tomatoes. For a spicy version, add a fresh green chili when you purée the vegetables, or a few drops of hot-pepper sauce before serving.

❧

*I*n a food processor fitted with the metal blade, combine the bread crumbs, olive oil and garlic and process until they form a smooth paste, stopping 2 or 3 times to scrape down the bowl. Set aside a small handful each of the onion, cucumber and bell pepper in a covered bowl in the refrigerator. Add the remaining onion, cucumber and bell pepper and all the tomatoes to the processor and process until smooth. Transfer to a bowl, cover tightly and refrigerate until well chilled, 2–3 hours. Chill serving bowls.

Using a whisk, stir in the tomato juice, water and vinegar. Season to taste with salt and white pepper. Ladle into the chilled bowls and garnish with the reserved vegetables, sour cream, croutons and chopped eggs.

Serves 6–8

Roasted Eggplant Soup with Mint

1½ lb (750 g) small- to medium-sized
  eggplants (aubergines)
2 tablespoons unsalted butter
1 small yellow onion, finely chopped
1 clove garlic, finely chopped
2½ cups (20 fl oz/625 ml) chicken stock
  or vegetable stock (recipes on pages
  8–11)
½ tablespoon finely chopped fresh mint
1 cup (8 fl oz/250 ml) heavy (double)
  cream
salt and white pepper
fresh mint sprigs for garnish

*Roasted eggplant develops a rich, earthy, slightly smoky flavor
that is highlighted in this simple soup. For an edge of sweetness,
swirl some puréed roasted red bell pepper (capsicum) into each
serving (see page 13). The soup may also be served chilled.*

Preheat an oven to 375°F (190°C).

  Put the eggplants in a baking dish and puncture their
skins several times with a fork. Roast in the oven, turning
occasionally, until the skins are evenly browned and deeply
wrinkled, 1–1½ hours. Let stand at room temperature until
cool enough to handle, then peel.

  In a large saucepan, melt the butter over medium heat.
Add the onion and garlic and sauté until golden, 3–5
minutes. Add the eggplants, breaking them up with a
wooden spoon, and sauté 2–3 minutes more. Add the stock
and mint and bring to a boil. Reduce the heat, cover and
simmer for about 20 minutes.

  In small batches, purée the soup in a food mill, a food
processor fitted with the metal blade or in a blender, taking
care to avoid splattering. Return the purée to the pan, stir in
the cream and gently heat through over low to medium
heat. Season to taste with salt and white pepper. Ladle into
warmed bowls and garnish with the mint sprigs.

Serves 4–6

Leek and Potato Soup

¼ cup (2 oz/60 g) unsalted butter

2 lb (1 kg) leeks, white portions only, trimmed, carefully washed and thinly sliced

6 cups (48 fl oz/1.5 l) chicken stock, vegetable stock (*recipes on pages 8–11*) or water

2 lb (1 kg) baking potatoes, peeled, quartered lengthwise and thinly sliced

salt and white pepper

2 tablespoons finely chopped fresh chives

You can make and serve this classic French soup in many different ways. Leave the vegetables whole and cook them in water alone for the most rustic version, enriched only with a little butter at serving time. For an even richer, more elegant variation, purée the soup in a food mill, food processor or blender, then stir in about 1 cup (8 fl oz/250 ml) light (single) cream and gently rewarm. Chill that creamy soup and you have a classic vichyssoise. The hot purée is also good with some shredded Swiss or Cheddar cheese stirred in at the last minute.

In a large saucepan, melt the butter over medium heat. Add the leeks and sauté just until they begin to soften, 3–5 minutes. Add the stock and potatoes, bring to a boil, reduce the heat to low, cover and simmer until the potatoes are very tender, about 20 minutes.

Season to taste with salt and white pepper. Ladle into warmed bowls and garnish with the chives.

Serves 8–10

Iced Melon Soup with Champagne and Ginger

5 cups (2½ lb/1.25 kg) coarsely chopped
  fresh cantaloupe or honeydew melon
1 tablespoon grated fresh ginger
1 tablespoon fresh lemon juice
3 cups (24 fl oz/750 ml) dry Champagne
  or sparkling wine, well chilled
1–2 tablespoons confectioners' (icing)
  sugar
fresh mint sprigs

Make this soup with the sweetest and juiciest cantaloupe or honeydew melon—whichever is available when you shop. For a special occasion, serve the soup in melon shells with decoratively cut edges. Sliced strawberries or whole raspberries make an attractive garnish. If you like serve with crisp plain cookies.

Purée the melon and ginger in a food mill. Or use a food processor fitted with the metal blade or a blender, taking care to avoid splattering. If you use a processor or blender, force the purée through a strainer set inside a bowl, pressing the solids with a wooden spoon. Stir in the lemon juice. Cover tightly and refrigerate until well chilled, at least 2 hours or for up to 12 hours. Chill serving bowls.

Just before serving, stir the Champagne or sparkling wine into the melon purée. Then stir in just enough of the sugar to emphasize the melon's flavor without making the soup overly sweet. Ladle into the chilled bowls and garnish with mint sprigs.

Serves 4–6

Stracciatella alla Fiorentina

6 cups (48 fl oz/1.5 l) chicken stock
  (recipe on page 8)
4 eggs
¼ cup (1 oz/30 g) freshly grated
  Parmesan cheese
1 cup (2 oz/60 g) packed thinly
  shredded spinach leaves

Stracciatella *means "little rag" in Italian, a fanciful description of
the shreds that form when egg and Parmesan cheese are stirred
into simmering stock to make this favorite Roman soup. The
addition of fresh spinach strips adds a Florentine touch. Pass
more Parmesan on the side for guests to add as they like. Omit
the cheese and spinach and stir in a splash of soy sauce mixed
with cornstarch (cornflour), and you have a simple Chinese egg
drop soup.*

In a large saucepan, bring the stock to a boil and reduce to a
brisk simmer.

   Meanwhile, in a bowl lightly beat the eggs and then stir in
the cheese. While stirring the stock constantly, drizzle in the
egg mixture and then add the spinach. Simmer 2–3 minutes
more and serve immediately.

Serves 4–6

Sausage and Black Bean Soup

3 cups (21 oz/655 g) dried black beans

1¾ lb (875 g) chorizo, andouille or other
   spicy sausages

1 tablespoon olive oil

4 cloves garlic, finely chopped

2 yellow onions, finely chopped

2 celery stalks, finely chopped

2½ qt (2.5 l) chicken stock or meat stock
   (recipes on pages 8–10)

4 tablespoons finely chopped fresh
   parsley

1 teaspoon dried oregano

½ teaspoon ground cumin

2 bay leaves

½ tablespoon salt

½ cup (4 fl oz/125 ml) sour cream

2 tablespoons finely chopped fresh
   chives

2 tablespoons finely chopped fresh
   cilantro (fresh coriander)

Throughout the Caribbean and parts of Latin America, black beans cooked to a thick, soupy consistency are enjoyed as an appetizer, or together with steamed white rice as a side dish or a simple main course. Substitute smoked ham, a ham hock or smoked turkey for the sausage. Or make a vegetarian version, using vegetable stock (recipe on page 11).

❉

Sort through the beans, discarding any impurities or discolored ones. Set aside.

Remove the casings from 1 lb (500 g) of the sausages. In a large saucepan, warm the oil over medium heat. Add the sausage meat and sauté, coarsely breaking up the meat with a wooden spoon, until lightly browned, about 5 minutes. Pour off all but about 3 tablespoons of the fat. Return the pan to the heat, add the garlic, onions and celery and sauté until the onions are translucent, 2–3 minutes.

Add the beans, stock, parsley, oregano, cumin and bay leaves and bring to a boil. Reduce the heat, cover and simmer gently until the beans are very tender, 2–2½ hours, adding half of the salt halfway through the cooking and adding a little water if necessary to keep the beans moist.

Discard the bay leaves. Pour a few ladlefuls of beans into a food mill, a food processor fitted with the metal blade or a blender; purée, taking care to avoid splattering. Stir back into the pan with the remaining salt. Taste and adjust the seasoning.

Cut the remaining sausages into slices ½ inch (12 mm) thick. Sauté in a nonstick frying pan over medium heat until browned, about 3 minutes per side. Ladle the soup into warmed bowls; garnish with the sour cream, sausage slices, chives and cilantro.

Serves 6–8

Classic Deli Matzo Ball Soup

3 qt (3 l) plus 1 cup (8 fl oz/250 ml) chicken stock (recipe on page 8)

2 large carrots, cut into 1-inch (2.5 cm) chunks

2 large celery stalks, cut into 1-inch (2.5-cm) chunks

1 large yellow onion, cut into 1-inch (2.5-cm) chunks

½ cup (¾ oz/20 g) coarsely chopped fresh parsley

2 cups (10 oz/300 g) matzo meal

8 eggs, separated

½ cup (4 fl oz/125 ml) rendered chicken fat or vegetable oil

1 teaspoon salt

½ teaspoon white pepper

Traditionally served at the Passover feast, this chicken broth with matzo-meal dumplings—crushed crackers of unleavened bread, available in Jewish delicatessens and the ethnic-food section of most supermarkets—is a year-round favorite. To add a little color to the matzo balls, stir 1–2 tablespoons finely chopped fresh parsley into the matzo-meal mixture. You can also make the matzo balls during the final simmering of freshly made chicken stock, and include shreds of boiled chicken in the soup along with the vegetables and dumplings. Serve with rye bread or toasted bagels.

❋

Put the 3 qt (3 l) stock in a medium to large pot with the carrots, celery, onion and parsley; you should have a depth of at least 4 inches (10 cm) of liquid for the matzo balls to float in. Bring to a boil over medium heat and reduce the heat to a bare simmer.

In a mixing bowl, combine the matzo meal, the 1 cup (8 fl oz/250 ml) stock, egg yolks, chicken fat or vegetable oil, salt and white pepper, stirring well. In a separate bowl, beat the egg whites with a whisk until very frothy but still liquid. Using a rubber spatula, fold the whites into the matzo-meal mixture until smoothly blended.

Moistening your hands with cold water, gently and quickly shape the matzo mixture into smooth balls 2–3 inches (5–7.5 cm) in diameter. As the balls are formed, gently drop them into the simmering soup. Cover partially and cook for about 30 minutes.

Ladle the stock into warmed bowls, adding matzo balls and a few pieces of vegetable and parsley to each portion.

Serves 8–10

Sweet-and-Sour Cabbage Soup with Flanken

¼ cup (2 fl oz/60 ml) vegetable oil

1 large yellow onion, coarsely chopped

2 cloves garlic, coarsely chopped

1 lb (500 g) flank steak, well trimmed of fat

salt and freshly ground pepper

8 cups (64 fl oz/2 l) meat stock (recipe on page 10) or water

1 can (1 lb/500 g) plum (Roma) tomatoes with their juice

⅓ cup (3 fl oz/80 ml) fresh lemon juice

¼ cup (2 oz/60 g) sugar

¼ cup (1 oz/30 g) golden or dark raisins

1 head Savoy cabbage, cored and cut into shreds ½ inch (12 mm) wide

2 bay leaves

4 tablespoons coarsely chopped fresh parsley, optional

A favorite preparation throughout Eastern Europe, this soup makes the most of economical flank steak—known in kosher butcher shops as flanken. You could substitute kielbasa sausages, cut into slices ½ inch (12 mm) thick and added to the pot with the cabbage. Serve with thick slices of rye bread.

❋

In a large pot, warm the oil over low to medium heat. Add the onion and garlic and sauté until translucent, 2–3 minutes. Lightly season the flank steak with salt and pepper, add to the pan and sauté, turning once, until lightly browned, 2–3 minutes on each side.

Add the stock and deglaze the pan by stirring and scraping to dislodge any browned bits. Add the tomatoes, crushing them slightly with a wooden spoon. Then add the lemon juice, sugar, raisins, cabbage and bay leaves. Raise the heat and bring to a boil. Reduce the heat to low, cover partially and simmer gently until the meat is tender, about 1 hour.

Discard the bay leaves. Remove the meat from the pot and, using a sharp knife and a fork, cut and tear it up into coarse, bite-sized shreds. Stir the shreds back into the pot. Taste the soup and adjust the seasoning. Ladle the soup into warmed bowls and garnish with the parsley, if desired.

Serves 8–10

Thai Spicy Chicken Soup with Lemongrass and Chilies

6 cups (48 fl oz/1.5 l) chicken stock
   (recipe on page 8)

6 dried lime leaves

2 stalks lemongrass, each about 8 inches
   (20 cm) long, cut into 1-inch (2.5-cm)
   pieces, or 2 long, thin strips lemon zest

2–4 small fresh hot green chili peppers,
   halved lengthwise

2–4 tablespoons Thai fish sauce

½–1 tablespoon hot chili oil

1 lb (500 g) boneless, skinless chicken
   breasts, cut crosswise into slices ¼ inch
   (6 mm) thick

1 can (15 oz/470 g) straw mushrooms,
   drained

about ½ cup (4 fl oz/125 ml) fresh lime
   juice

½ cup (¾ oz/20 g) coarsely torn fresh
   cilantro (fresh coriander) leaves,
   optional

A Thai-restaurant standby, this simple clear soup, called tom yum kai, *makes a satisfying light meal when served with steamed rice. The seasonings—dried lime leaves and lemongrass—are readily available in Southeast Asian food stores; if you can't find them, substitute strips of fresh lemon peel. You will also find the fish sauce, called* nam pla, *in Thai or other Asian shops, specialty markets and some well-stocked food markets. Medium-sized whole shrimp (prawns), peeled and deveined, may be substituted for the chicken. For an attractive presentation, all the seasonings are left in the stock; be sure to warn your guests not to eat them—especially the chilies.*

❀

Put the stock, lime leaves and lemongrass or lemon zest in a saucepan and bring to a boil over medium heat. Reduce the heat to low and simmer, uncovered, for about 10 minutes. Add the chilies and simmer for 5 minutes more.

Stir in the fish sauce and chili oil to taste, then add the chicken strips and straw mushrooms. Simmer gently, skimming any froth from the surface, until the chicken is cooked through, about 5 minutes. Stir in the lime juice to taste, immediately ladle into warmed bowls and garnish with the cilantro, if desired.

Serves 4–6

Lamb and Chick-pea Soup

1¼ cups (8 oz/250 g) dried chick-peas (garbanzo beans)

2 tablespoons olive oil

1½ lb (750 g) lamb shoulder, in one piece

salt and freshly ground pepper

1 yellow onion, finely chopped

1 carrot, finely chopped

1 clove garlic, finely chopped

¾ teaspoon ground coriander

¾ teaspoon ground cumin

¼ teaspoon cayenne pepper

5 cups (40 fl oz/1.25 l) meat stock or chicken stock *(recipes on pages 8–10)*

2 large plum (Roma) tomatoes, coarsely chopped

3 large lemons, cut into quarters

2 green (spring) onions, including tender green parts, thinly sliced

4 tablespoons coarsely chopped fresh parsley

This rustic soup is inspired by North African cooking. Beef short ribs may be substituted for the lamb.

❀

Sort through the chick-peas, discarding any impurities or discolored ones. Place the chick-peas in a bowl, add cold water to cover and leave to soak for about 12 hours.

In a large pot, heat the oil over medium heat. Season the lamb with salt and pepper and sauté until evenly browned, 3–4 minutes on each side. Remove the lamb and set it aside. Pour off all but about 2 tablespoons of the fat.

Add the onion, carrot and garlic and sauté over medium heat until the onion is translucent, 2–3 minutes. Add the coriander, cumin and cayenne and sauté for 1 minute more. Pour in the stock and deglaze the pot by stirring to dislodge any browned bits. Return the lamb to the pot. Drain the chick-peas and add them to the pot along with the tomatoes. Add 4 lemon quarters. Bring to a boil, reduce the heat to low, cover and simmer gently until the lamb and chick-peas are tender, 2–2½ hours, skimming regularly.

Remove the lamb from the pot. Cut out and discard the bones and excess fat; cut the meat into small, coarse chunks and set aside. Discard the lemon quarters. Ladle about half of the chick-peas into a food mill, a processor fitted with the metal blade or a blender and purée, taking care to avoid splattering. Stir the purée and lamb chunks back into the pot. Taste and adjust the seasoning.

Ladle into warmed bowls, garnish with the green onions and parsley and pass the remaining lemon wedges on the side.

Serves 6–8

Turkey and Root Vegetable Soup

2 large carrots, cut into slices ½ inch (12 mm) thick

2 large parsnips, cut into slices ½ inch (12 mm) thick

2 large boiling potatoes, cut into slices ½ inch (12 mm) thick

2 large yellow onions, thickly sliced

2 bay leaves

½ cup (¾ oz/20 g) coarsely chopped fresh parsley

1 tablespoon dried thyme

1 roast turkey carcass, with any meat attached, broken into 6 or so large pieces

2½ qt (2.5 l) chicken stock (*recipe on page 8*)

salt and freshly ground pepper

When you roast a holiday turkey, refrigerate the carcass for use a day or two later in this easy, robust soup; chicken carcasses may be substituted for the turkey. The soup may also be made using 2 pounds (1 kg) of fresh turkey pieces such as drumsticks or thighs; just add them when you would add the carcass. You can vary the staple autumn vegetables according to what is available. If you like, 15 minutes before serving, boil about ½ pound (250 g) wide egg noodles in a separate pan of water, drain well and add to the soup; or serve the soup over steamed white or brown rice.

❧

*I*n a large pot, combine all the vegetables, the bay leaves, parsley and thyme. Arrange the turkey carcass pieces on top and pour in the stock. Bring to a boil over medium heat, skimming away the froth from the surface. Reduce the heat, cover and simmer gently, skimming occasionally, until the vegetables are very tender, 45–60 minutes.

Discard the bay leaves. Using a slotted spoon, remove the carcass pieces. Pick off any meat clinging to the bones and return the meat to the pot. Season to taste with salt and pepper and ladle into warmed bowls.

Serves 10–12

Hungarian Pork Goulash Soup

¼ cup (2 oz/60 g) unsalted butter

2 tablespoons vegetable oil

1 yellow onion, finely chopped

2 cloves garlic, finely chopped

1 lb (500 g) pork tenderloin, trimmed
of fat and cut into ¼- to ½-inch
(6- to 12-mm) cubes

2 tablespoons hot paprika

½ tablespoon caraway seeds

8 cups (64 fl oz/2 l) meat stock *(recipe on
page 10)*

1 cup (8 fl oz/250 ml) dry white wine

2 boiling potatoes, peeled and cut into
¼- to ½-inch (6- to 12-mm) cubes

salt and freshly ground pepper

¾ cup (6 fl oz/180 ml) sour cream

4 tablespoons chopped fresh chives

True Hungarian gulyas *is a rustic peasant soup or stew of red
meat, onions and potato, seasoned with earthy-hot paprika—its
unmistakable signature—and caraway seeds. If you want
something even more substantial, serve the soup over cooked egg
noodles. If you like, add some diced bell pepper (capsicum) with
the onion, or stir in a generous tablespoon of tomato paste with
the stock. Beef steak may be substituted for the pork.*

❀

*I*n a large saucepan, warm the butter and oil over medium
heat. Add the onion and garlic and sauté until the onion is
translucent, 2–3 minutes. Raise the heat, add the pork and
sauté until it is lightly browned, 3–5 minutes. Sprinkle in
the paprika and caraway seeds and sauté for 1 minute more.

Add the stock, wine and potatoes. Bring to a boil and
deglaze the pan by stirring to dislodge any browned bits.
Reduce the heat and simmer, uncovered, until the pork and
potatoes are tender, about 30 minutes.

Season to taste with salt and pepper, ladle into warmed
bowls and garnish with the sour cream and chives.

Serves 6–8

Japanese Miso Ramen with Sliced Pork and Egg

½ cup (4 fl oz/125 ml) Japanese *mirin*

2 tablespoons soy sauce

1 lb (500 g) boneless pork loin, trimmed of fat

2½ qt (2.5 l) meat stock or chicken stock (recipes on pages 8–10)

4 slices fresh ginger, each about ¼ inch (6 mm) thick

1 lb (500 g) dried Japanese *ramen* noodles

¼ cup (3 oz/90 g) Japanese red or white *miso* paste

1½ cups (2½ oz/75 g) coarsely shredded spinach leaves

1½ cups (6 oz/185 g) mung bean sprouts

2 eggs, hard cooked and cut into quarters lengthwise

½ cup (1½ oz/45 g) thinly sliced green (spring) onions, including tender green parts

All over Japan, and in Japanese enclaves throughout the world, ramen shops serve up nothing but large bowls filled with steaming broth, wheat noodles (ramen) and a wide range of toppings. This recipe calls for some of the most common garnishes; other options include sliced canned bamboo shoots, cooked corn kernels, diced bean curd (tofu) and stir-fried vegetables. Mirin is a sweet rice wine commonly used in Japanese cooking.

❉

*I*n a mixing bowl, stir together the *mirin* and soy sauce. Turn the pork in the mixture to coat well. Cover tightly and refrigerate for 1 hour, turning 2 or 3 more times.

Put the stock and ginger in a large saucepan and bring to a boil. Reduce the heat to low. Remove the pork from its marinade and add it to the pot. Cover partially and poach in the barely simmering liquid until tender, about 1 hour; skim the surface frequently. About 10 minutes before the pork is done, bring a separate saucepan of water to a boil and cook the *ramen* until tender, 3–4 minutes. Drain well.

Remove the pork from the stock; discard the ginger. Using a sharp knife, carve the pork into slices ¼ inch (6 mm) thick. Stir the *miso* into the stock until it dissolves completely.

Divide the *ramen* among 4 large serving bowls, mounding them in the center. Ladle in the stock. Scatter the spinach along the edges of each bowl, immersing the shreds in the stock. Arrange the sliced pork, bean sprouts and egg quarters in the center. Scatter the green onions on top.

Serves 4

Mulligatawny with Tandoori-Style Chicken and Mint Raita

FOR THE CHICKEN:
½ cup (4 oz/125 g) plain low-fat yogurt
1 tablespoon fresh lemon juice
½ tablespoon curry powder
1 teaspoon sweet paprika
1 lb (500 g) skinless, boneless chicken
    breasts
salt and freshly ground pepper

FOR THE SOUP:
2 tablespoons vegetable oil
2 tablespoons unsalted butter
1 yellow onion, finely chopped
1 clove garlic, finely chopped
1 hot fresh green chili pepper, seeded
    and finely chopped
1 teaspoon grated fresh ginger
1 tablespoon curry powder
6 cups (48 fl oz/1.5 l) chicken stock
    (recipe on page 8)
4 plum (Roma) tomatoes, peeled, seeded
    and finely chopped
1 large tart green apple, cored, peeled
    and finely chopped
1 carrot, coarsely chopped
salt and freshly ground pepper

FOR THE RAITA:
½ cup (4 oz/125 g) plain low-fat yogurt
2 tablespoons finely shredded fresh mint
    leaves
1 tablespoon fresh lemon juice

The name for this Indian-style soup derives from milakutanni, Tamil *for "pepper water." While it is excellent made without chicken or with leftover cooked chicken, freshly broiled chicken breasts add extra elegance.*

❋

*F*or the chicken, in a mixing bowl stir together the yogurt, lemon juice, curry powder and paprika. Turn the chicken breasts in this mixture, cover tightly and refrigerate for 30–60 minutes.

In a large saucepan, warm the oil and butter over medium heat. Add the onion, garlic, chili and ginger; sauté until translucent, 2–3 minutes. Stir in the curry powder and sauté for 1 minute more. Add the stock, tomatoes, apple and carrot and bring to a boil. Reduce the heat, cover and simmer for about 30 minutes.

Meanwhile, preheat a broiler (griller) or a gas or electric grill until very hot. About 10 minutes before serving, remove the chicken from the yogurt and season to taste with salt and pepper. Cook close to the heat source, turning once, until cooked through and golden brown, 4–5 minutes per side.

While the chicken is cooking, prepare the *raita* by stirring together the yogurt, mint and lemon juice.

Before serving the soup, taste and adjust the seasoning. Cut the chicken crosswise into slices ¼ inch (6 mm) thick. Ladle the soup into warmed shallow soup plates. Spoon in the *raita* and arrange the chicken on top.

Serves 6–8

77

Albóndigas with Beef-and-Tortilla Meatballs

1 lb (500 g) lean ground (minced) beef
4 eggs, lightly beaten
½ small red (Spanish) onion, finely chopped
¾ cup (3 oz/90 g) crushed tortilla chips
4 tablespoons finely chopped fresh cilantro (fresh coriander)
1 tablespoon dried oregano
1 teaspoon salt
½ teaspoon ground cumin
½ teaspoon freshly ground pepper
7 cups (56 fl oz/1.75 l) meat stock or chicken stock (recipes on pages 8–10)
1 can (1 lb/500 g) tomatoes with their juice
2 teaspoons sugar
1 teaspoon red pepper flakes
2 carrots, coarsely chopped
2 celery stalks, coarsely chopped
1 onion, coarsely chopped
1 bay leaf

The Mexican word albóndigas *refers both to the savory meatballs and the vegetable soup in which they are cooked and served. Ground (minced) pork or turkey may be substituted for the beef. Serve with warm corn tortillas.*

❉

In a mixing bowl, stir together the beef, eggs, onion, tortilla chips, cilantro, oregano, salt, cumin and pepper. Cover tightly and refrigerate for 1 hour.

Put the stock in a large saucepan. Add the tomatoes, crushing them slightly with a wooden spoon, along with the sugar, red pepper flakes, carrots, celery, onion and bay leaf. Bring to a boil and reduce the heat to a simmer.

Moistening your hands with cold water, form the beef mixture into balls 1–1½ inches (2.5–4 cm) in diameter and slip them carefully into the simmering stock. Cover and simmer gently until the meatballs are cooked through and the vegetables are tender, about 20 minutes.

Discard the bay leaf. Taste the stock and adjust the seasoning. Ladle into warmed bowls and serve.

Serves 8–10

Greek Chicken and Lemon Soup with Orzo

8 cups (64 fl oz/2 l) chicken stock (*recipe on page 8*)

¾ cup (4 oz/125 g) orzo or other rice-shaped pasta

1 boneless, skinless chicken breast, ½ lb (250 g), cut crosswise into slices ¼ inch (6 mm) thick

3 eggs

⅓ cup (3 fl oz/80 ml) fresh lemon juice

1 tablespoon grated lemon zest

salt and white pepper

2 tablespoons finely chopped fresh parsley

This fresh-tasting Greek soup, known as avgolemono, *is based on chicken stock, thickened and flavored with a mixture of beaten egg and lemon juice. If you cannot find orzo or similar rice-shaped pasta, substitute an equal amount of long-grain white rice. Serve with toasted pita or hunks of sesame bread.*

❋

*I*n a large saucepan, bring the stock to a boil over medium heat. Reduce the heat to medium-low, add the orzo or other pasta and cook, uncovered, until very tender, 15–20 minutes. About 5 minutes before the pasta is done, add the chicken breast slices.

Place the eggs in a mixing bowl. Whisk the eggs while pouring in the lemon juice. Stir in the zest. Whisking continuously, slowly pour a ladleful of the hot stock into the egg mixture. Reduce the heat to very low. Then, while whisking the soup in the pan, slowly pour in the egg mixture; the soup should thicken slightly.

Season to taste with salt and white pepper. Remove from the heat, ladle immediately into warmed bowls and garnish with the parsley.

Serves 6–8

Chinese Hot-and-Sour Soup with Duck

¼ cup (1 oz/30 g) small dried black tree fungus

2 tablespoons dried lily buds

6 dried shiitake mushrooms

1 boneless, skinless duck breast, 4–6 oz (125–185 g)

2 tablespoons soy sauce

2 tablespoons cornstarch (cornflour)

2 teaspoons Asian sesame oil

½ tablespoon freshly ground pepper

1 teaspoon Chinese rice wine or dry sherry

½ teaspoon sugar

5 cups (40 fl oz/1.25 l) chicken stock (*recipe on page 8*)

½ lb (250 g) firm bean curd (tofu), well drained and cut into ½-inch (12-mm) cubes

⅓ cup (3 fl oz/80 ml) rice vinegar or cider vinegar

½–1 teaspoon hot chili oil

1 egg, beaten

2 large green (spring) onions, including tender green parts, thinly sliced

One of the great specialties of Chinese cuisine, hot-and-sour soup may also be made with lean pork loin, beef steak or chicken breast in place of the duck used here. All the special ingredients are readily found in Asian food shops. A large bowlful makes a satisfying lunch in itself.

❀

*P*ut the tree fungus, lily buds and shiitake mushrooms in separate bowls and cover each generously with cold water. Leave to soak for about 30 minutes.

Using a sharp knife, cut the duck breast lengthwise into thin slices. Cut the slices lengthwise into thin strips, then cut the strips crosswise into pieces about 2 inches (5 cm) long. In a bowl combine half each of the soy sauce, cornstarch, sesame oil and pepper with the wine and sugar. Add the duck shreds, toss and marinate at room temperature for 15–30 minutes.

Drain the tree fungus, lily buds and shiitakes and rinse well to remove any grit. Cut off and discard the shiitake stems. Cut the tree fungus and shiitakes into thin strips; leave the lily buds whole.

In a large saucepan, bring the stock to a boil over medium heat; reduce the heat until the stock simmers. Add the bean curd, tree fungus, lily buds and shiitakes. In a small bowl, stir together the vinegar, chili oil and the remaining soy sauce and cornstarch until smoothly blended; stir into the stock along with the duck strips and their marinade and the remaining pepper. Pour in the egg and stir immediately so it forms thin wisps. Stir in the remaining sesame oil, ladle immediately into warmed bowls and garnish generously with the green onions.

Serves 4–6

Steamed Clams in Garlic Seafood Broth

4 dozen clams in the shell, well scrubbed
  (see glossary, page 105)
1 tablespoon olive oil
4 cloves garlic, minced
4 cups (32 fl oz/1 l) fish stock (recipe on
  page 9)
1 cup (8 fl oz/250 ml) dry white wine
2 tablespoons unsalted butter
4 tablespoons coarsely chopped fresh
  parsley
2 large lemons, cut into wedges

Both a simple soup and a classic seafood appetizer, this dish satisfies shellfish lovers with its utter simplicity. Try cooking fresh mussels the same way. Serve with plenty of crusty bread to sop up the broth.

✳

Discard any cracked or open clams.

In a large pot, warm the oil over low to medium heat. Add the garlic and sauté until translucent, 1–2 minutes. Then add the stock and wine, raise the heat and bring to a boil. Reduce the heat slightly, add the clams, cover and steam just until they open, 7–10 minutes.

Line a strainer with cheesecloth (muslin) and set inside a large bowl. Pour the contents of the pot into the bowl; discard any unopened clams.

Return the strained liquid to the pot over medium heat. Add the butter and parsley and stir until the butter melts. Arrange the clams in warmed shallow soup plates and ladle the broth over them. Serve with the lemon wedges.

Serves 6–8

Cream of Shrimp

3 tablespoons unsalted butter

2 carrots, finely chopped

1 yellow onion, finely chopped

1 celery stalk, finely chopped

1 small baking potato, peeled and finely chopped

2 lb (1 kg) small shrimp (prawns), peeled and deveined, shells reserved

2 cups (16 fl oz/500 ml) fish stock (*recipe on page 9*)

2 cups (16 fl oz/500 ml) light (single) cream

½ tablespoon dried thyme

1 bay leaf, crumbled

salt and white pepper

1 tablespoon fresh chervil or parsley leaves

A few aromatic vegetables, simple herbs and cream highlight the natural sweetness of shrimp in this rich yet light-bodied soup. For a spicier version, stir in some cayenne pepper to taste.

In a large saucepan, melt the butter over medium heat. Add the carrots, onion, celery, potato and shrimp shells and sauté until the onion is translucent and the shells turn pink, 2–3 minutes.

Add the stock, cream, thyme, bay leaf and all but a handful of the shelled shrimp. Bring to a boil, reduce the heat, cover and simmer gently for about 20 minutes.

In small batches, purée the soup in a food mill. Or purée in a food processor fitted with the metal blade or in a blender, taking care to guard against splattering. If you use a processor or blender, force the purée through a strainer, pressing the solids with a wooden spoon. Return the soup to the pan and season to taste with salt and white pepper.

Cut the remaining shrimp into small chunks and add to the soup. Simmer gently until cooked through, 2–3 minutes. Garnish with the chervil or parsley.

Serves 4–6

Consommé with Grilled Seafood

6 cups (48 fl oz/1.5 l) fish stock (*recipe on page 9*)

½ lb (250 g) sea scallops

½ lb (250 g) shrimp (prawns), peeled and deveined

2 tablespoons unsalted butter, melted

salt and white pepper

fresh chives, cut into 1-inch (2.5-cm) lengths

Serve this soup at the start of an elegant dinner. If your market has fresh shiitake mushrooms, add them, grilling them along with the seafood.

✳

Preheat a broiler (griller) or a gas or electric grill until very hot. Or prepare a fire in a charcoal grill.

In a saucepan, bring the fish stock to a boil over medium heat. Reduce the heat to very low and cover the pan.

Meanwhile, brush the scallops and shrimp with the melted butter and season lightly with salt and white pepper. Place them on a broiler tray or on a grill rack and cook close to the heat source until well seared and barely cooked through, 1–2 minutes per side.

When the seafood is almost done, ladle the hot stock into warmed large, shallow soup plates, taking care not to fill them all the way. Neatly place the seafood in the stock; they should protrude slightly above the surface of the liquid. Float the chives in the stock and serve immediately.

Serves 4–6

New England Clam Chowder with Leeks and Bacon

3 dozen clams in the shell, well scrubbed
   (*see glossary, page 105*)
2 tablespoons unsalted butter
1 clove garlic, minced
2 cups (16 fl oz/500 ml) water
1 cup (8 fl oz/250 ml) dry white wine
¼ lb (125 g) lean bacon, rind removed,
   coarsely chopped
1 leek, including tender green parts,
   trimmed, carefully washed and thinly
   sliced
1 tablespoon all-purpose (plain) flour
2 cups (16 fl oz/500 ml) light (single)
   cream
1 lb (500 g) red potatoes, peeled or
   unpeeled, cut into ½-inch (12-mm)
   cubes
¾ teaspoon dried thyme
freshly ground black pepper
1 tablespoon finely chopped fresh chives
1 tablespoon finely chopped fresh
   parsley

The slightly sweet flavors of the leeks and bacon highlight the natural sweetness of fresh clams in this elaboration of a classic chowder. Fresh bay scallops would also be good prepared this way. Serve with crusty bread or oyster crackers.

✳

Discard any cracked or open clams. In a large pot, melt 1 table-spoon of the butter over low to medium heat. Add the garlic and sauté until it begins to soften, 1–2 minutes. Add the water and wine, raise the heat and bring to a boil. Reduce the heat slightly. Immediately add the clams, cover and steam just until they open, 7–10 minutes.

Line a strainer with cheesecloth (muslin) and set inside a large bowl. Empty the pot into the strainer; discard any unopened clams. Set the clams and strained liquid aside separately.

Rinse out the pot, add the remaining butter and place over medium heat. Add the bacon and sauté until it just begins to brown. Add the leek and sauté until it begins to soften, 2–3 minutes. Sprinkle in the flour and cook, stirring, 1 minute more.

Stirring continuously, pour in the reserved clam liquid and the cream. When the liquid reaches a boil, reduce the heat to a simmer. Add the potatoes and thyme.

Pull the clams from the shells. If they are large, cut them into ½-inch (12-mm) pieces. When the potatoes are tender, after about 15 minutes, add the clams and simmer for 1–2 minutes more. Season to taste with pepper. Ladle into warmed bowls and garnish with the chives and parsley.

Serves 4–6

Provençal Fish Soup

½ teaspoon saffron threads
salt
3 tablespoons olive oil
3 cloves garlic, finely chopped
1 yellow onion, finely chopped
1 leek, including tender green parts,
   trimmed, carefully washed and thinly
   sliced
½ cup (2½ oz/75 g) diced celery
¼ teaspoon hot paprika
3 boiling potatoes, cut into cubes
3 tomatoes, peeled and coarsely chopped
3 fresh parsley sprigs
2 fresh thyme sprigs
2 long, thin strips orange zest
1 bay leaf
5 cups (40 fl oz/1.25 l) water
1 cup (8 fl oz/250 ml) dry white wine
freshly ground pepper
2½ lb (1.25 kg) assorted white fish
   fillets, such as red snapper, sea bass,
   halibut or lingcod, cut into 1- to 2-inch
   (2.5- to 5-cm) pieces

With its aromatic combination of saffron, olive oil, garlic and tomatoes, this quickly made soup resembles the traditional bouillabaisse of the south of France. Use whatever fresh white fish is available, in whatever combination you like. For a more elaborate version, add fresh shrimp (prawns) or scallops. And as a final serving flourish, rub thin slices of dry French bread with garlic, brush with olive oil and bake in the oven until crisp and golden, then float them in individual servings of the soup.

✳

P̲ut the saffron threads and a pinch of salt in a metal kitchen spoon. Hold the spoon over heat for a few seconds, then use the back of a teaspoon to crush the threads into a powder. Set aside.

Warm the oil in a large pot over medium heat. Add the garlic, onion, leek, celery and paprika and sauté, stirring continuously, for 2–3 minutes. Add the potatoes, tomatoes, parsley, thyme, orange zest and bay leaf. Cook for 5 minutes more, stirring occasionally. Add the crushed saffron, water, wine and salt and pepper to taste. Cover and simmer for about 15 minutes.

Add the fish to the pot and simmer, uncovered, until cooked through, 10–15 minutes more, adding more water, if necessary, to keep the fish covered.

Discard the bay leaf. Adjust the seasoning and serve in warmed bowls.

Serves 4–6

Sherried Crab Bisque

¼ cup (2 oz/60 g) unsalted butter

2 shallots, finely chopped

1 large yellow onion, finely chopped

1 large carrot, finely chopped

1 celery stalk, finely chopped

1 bay leaf, crumbled

1 teaspoon finely chopped fresh tarragon
   or ½ teaspoon dried tarragon

2 whole steamed cracked crabs, meat
   removed and flaked, shells broken into
   several pieces and reserved

¾ cup (6 fl oz/180 ml) dry sherry

2 cups (16 fl oz/500 ml) dry white wine

2 cups (16 fl oz/500 ml) water

2 cups (16 fl oz/500 ml) heavy (double)
   cream

1½ cups (3 oz/90 g) fine fresh bread
   crumbs

salt and white pepper

1 tablespoon finely chopped fresh chives
   or tarragon

A good seafood merchant will be able to sell you already cooked, cracked crab in the shell. The shells are essential to enhance the flavor and color of the soup. You can also make the bisque with shrimp (prawns) or lobster. If you prefer thyme, substitute it for the tarragon.

*I*n a large, heavy saucepan, melt the butter over low to medium heat. Add the shallots, onion, carrot, celery, bay leaf and tarragon. Sauté until the vegetables begin to soften, 5–7 minutes. Add the crab shells and sauté, stirring constantly, about 5 minutes more.

Add the sherry, raise the heat slightly, stir briefly and then add the white wine, water and half of the crab meat. Bring to a boil, reduce the heat and simmer briskly until the liquid reduces by about half, about 20 minutes.

Remove the crab shell pieces and discard. Empty the pan contents into a food mill set inside a bowl; purée. Alternatively, pour the contents into a fine-mesh strainer set inside a bowl and press with a wooden spoon to extract all the liquid. Discard the solids.

Rinse the saucepan, return the liquid to it and bring to a boil. Reduce the heat to low and stir in the cream, then the bread crumbs. Simmer briskly until thick, stirring occasionally, about 10 minutes more. Stir in the reserved crab meat, simmer about 5 minutes more, and season to taste with salt and white pepper. Ladle into warmed bowls and garnish with the chives or tarragon.

Serves 4–6

Scallops à la Nage

3 cups (24 fl oz/750 ml) fish stock (*recipe on page 9*) or water
3 cups (24 fl oz/750 ml) dry white wine
1 small leek, including tender green parts, trimmed, carefully washed and thinly sliced
1 small yellow onion, finely diced
1 small carrot, finely diced
1 small celery stalk, finely diced
salt and white pepper
1 lb (500 g) bay scallops
fresh chervil or parsley sprigs

The French phrase à la nage *translates as "in the swim," describing the light bath of white wine, water or fish stock and vegetables in which the little bay scallops are quickly poached and served. You can cook crayfish, shrimp (prawns) or strips of fish fillet in the same way.*

✳

In a large saucepan, combine the stock or water, wine, leek, onion, carrot and celery. Bring to a boil over medium heat. Reduce the heat to low and simmer gently, uncovered, skimming off any froth that forms on the surface, until the vegetables are tender, about 10 minutes. Season to taste with salt and white pepper.

Add the scallops and simmer just until cooked through, 2–3 minutes. Ladle into warmed shallow soup plates or bowls and garnish with chervil or parsley.

Serves 4–6

Seafood and Okra Gumbo

⅓ cup (3 fl oz/80 ml) vegetable oil

1 yellow onion, coarsely chopped

2 cloves garlic, finely chopped

3 tablespoons all-purpose (plain) flour

4 cups (32 fl oz/1 l) fish stock, heated
(recipe on page 9)

1 can (1 lb/500 g) plum (Roma)
tomatoes with their juice

1 lb (500 g) cooked lump crab meat,
coarsely flaked

½ lb (250 g) okra, trimmed and cut into
½-inch (12-mm) pieces, or ½ lb (250 g)
frozen cut okra

1 green bell pepper (capsicum), seeded,
deribbed and diced

2 bay leaves

1 teaspoon dried basil

1 teaspoon dried oregano

1 teaspoon dried thyme

1–2 teaspoons hot-pepper sauce, plus
extra for serving

salt and freshly ground pepper

1 lb (500 g) shrimp (prawns), peeled
and deveined

2 cups (14 oz/440 g) long-grain white
rice, steamed

You can make a meal of this hearty Louisiana soup, which is literally a melting pot of Creole and Cajun cultures. A descendant of French bouillabaisse, it includes the okra brought over by Africans and a spicy dose of New World chilies. If you like, add chicken, diced ham or andouille sausage with the crab meat, and freshly shucked oysters with the shrimp.

✳

In a large, heavy saucepan, warm the oil over low to medium heat. Add the onion and garlic and sauté until translucent, 2–3 minutes. Reduce the heat to low, sprinkle in the flour and continue sautéing, stirring occasionally, until the flour turns hazelnut brown, about 5 minutes more.

Whisking continuously, slowly stir in the stock. Add the tomatoes, crushing them slightly with a wooden spoon. Then add the crab meat, okra, bell pepper, bay leaves, basil, oregano, thyme and hot-pepper sauce. Raise the heat and bring to a boil. Reduce the heat to low, cover partially and simmer until thick but still fairly liquid, about 1 hour.

Before serving, taste the gumbo and season to taste with salt, pepper and, if you like, more hot-pepper sauce. Stir in the shrimp and simmer until they turn pink and are cooked through, about 5 minutes more.

Mound some of the rice in the center of individual soup bowls. Ladle the gumbo over it. Pass extra hot-pepper sauce on the side.

Serves 8–10

Oyster Cream Soup

¼ cup (2 oz/60 g) unsalted butter

1 boiling potato, peeled and cut into ¼-inch (6-mm) dice

1 carrot, cut into ¼-inch (6-mm) dice

1 celery stalk, cut into ¼-inch (6-mm) dice

1 small onion, finely chopped

3 cups (1½ lb/750 g) shucked (open) oysters in their liquor

2 cups (16 fl oz/500 ml) milk

2 cups (16 fl oz/500 ml) light (single) cream

1 teaspoon finely chopped fresh thyme

½–1 teaspoon hot-pepper sauce

salt and freshly ground pepper

1 tablespoon chopped fresh chives

The distinctive, briny taste of fresh oysters and their liquor—the liquid in their shells—needs only a few simple embellishments to produce a rich-tasting soup. Many fish markets will sell you already shucked fresh oysters in their liquor. Sauté a few chopped strips of bacon along with the vegetables, if you like. Serve with oyster crackers or buttered toast.

✳

In a large saucepan, melt the butter over low to medium heat. Add the potato, carrot, celery and onion and sauté until the onion is translucent, 2–3 minutes. Pour the oyster liquor through a fine-mesh strainer into the pan, then add the milk, cream and thyme. Bring to a boil, reduce the heat to low and simmer gently, uncovered, stirring frequently, until the vegetables are tender, 7–10 minutes.

Add the oysters and cook just until they turn tan and their edges curl, 2–3 minutes more. Season to taste with hot-pepper sauce, salt and pepper. Ladle into warmed shallow soup plates and garnish with the chives.

Serves 4–6

Baja Seafood Chowder

2 tablespoons olive oil
2 cloves garlic, finely chopped
1 yellow onion, finely chopped
1 large green bell pepper (capsicum),
    seeded, deribbed and coarsely
    chopped
1 fresh jalapeño chili pepper, seeded and
    finely chopped
1 teaspoon red pepper flakes
1 cup (8 fl oz/250 ml) fish stock (*recipe
    on page 9*)
¼ cup (2 fl oz/60 ml) dry red wine
2 cans (1 lb/500 g each) tomatoes,
    coarsely chopped, with their juice
2 tablespoons tomato paste
1½ tablespoons sugar
1 teaspoon dried oregano
1 teaspoon dried basil
1 bay leaf
1 baking potato, peeled and cut into
    ½-inch (12-mm) pieces
salt and freshly ground pepper
12 small clams in the shell, well
    scrubbed (*see glossary, page 105*)
½ lb (250 g) swordfish or sea bass fillets,
    cut into 1- to 2-inch (2.5- to 5-cm)
    pieces
½ lb (250 g) small- to medium-sized
    shrimp (prawns), peeled and deveined
½ cup (¾ oz/20 g) finely chopped fresh
    cilantro (fresh coriander)
2 limes, cut into wedges

A hint of hot chili pepper, cilantro and lime juice add a south-of-the-border spark to this variation on a Manhattan-style red seafood chowder. Use whatever fresh seafood looks good at the market; scallops, lump crab meat and mussels make good additions. And feel free to cut down on the spice if you like. Crusty garlic bread is a good accompaniment.

✳

In a large pot, heat the oil over medium heat. Add the garlic, onion, bell pepper, jalapeño and pepper flakes. Sauté until the onion is translucent, 2–3 minutes. Add the stock, wine, tomatoes, tomato paste, sugar, oregano, basil, bay leaf and potato. Bring to a boil, reduce the heat, cover and simmer, stirring occasionally, until the soup is thick but still fairly liquid, about 30 minutes.

Season to taste with salt and pepper. Discard any clams that are cracked or open. Add the clams to the pot, along with the fish and shrimp. Raise the heat slightly, cover and cook until the fish flakes, the shrimp turn pink and the clams open, 7–10 minutes. Discard any clams that do not open during cooking.

Ladle into warmed bowls, garnish with the cilantro and pass the lime wedges at the table.

Serves 8–10

Glossary

The following glossary defines terms both generally and specifically as they relate to soup and its preparation. Included are major and unusual ingredients and techniques.

BASIL
Sweet, spicy herb popular in Italian and French cooking, particularly as a seasoning for **tomatoes.**

BAY LEAVES
Dried whole leaves of the bay laurel tree, which add a pungent and spicy undertone when simmered in soups. The French variety, sometimes available in specialty-food shops, has a milder, sweeter flavor than California bay leaves. Remove the leaves from soup or other dish before serving.

BEAN CURD
Also known as tofu. Soft, custard-like curd, made from milky liquid extracted from fresh soybeans, caused to solidify by a coagulating agent. Popular throughout Asia, fresh bean curd is widely available in Asian food stores as well as in some supermarkets.

BLACK TREE FUNGUS
Small dried black fungus, also known as wood ear, tree ear or other similar names for its small, earlike shape. Popular in Chinese cooking, it has little flavor but is prized for its lustrous color and crunchy texture. Before use, it must be soaked in water. Available in Asian food stores and well-stocked food markets.

BEANS
All kinds of dried beans may be added to or used as the main ingredient of robust soups. Before use, they should be carefully picked over to remove any impurities such as small stones or fibers or any discolored or misshapen beans. Next, to rehydrate them and thus ensure even and thorough cooking, whole beans are often presoaked in enough cold water to cover them well for at least 8 hours or preferably 12 hours. All beans also require full boiling at the beginning of cooking—peas just briefly, beans for up to 10 minutes—to neutralize natural toxins they contain.

Dozens of different kinds of beans are used in cuisines worldwide; some of the more common varieties used in soups include:

Baby Lima Beans
Small variety of flat, white, kidney-shaped beans with a mild flavor and soft texture. Larger dried lima beans may be substituted.

Black Beans
Earthy-tasting, mealy-textured beans, relatively small in size and with deep black skins. Also called turtle beans.

Black-eyed Peas
Small, bean-shaped peas, rich in flavor and with a distinctive black dot on their otherwise ivory skins.

Cannellini Beans
Italian variety of small, white, thin-skinned, oval beans. Great Northern or white (navy) beans may be substituted.

Chick-peas
Round, tan-colored member of the pea family, with a slightly crunchy texture and nutlike flavor. Also known as garbanzo beans or *ceci* beans.

Kidney Beans
Widely popular, kidney-shaped beans with brownish red skins, slightly mealy texture and robust flavor. White kidney beans are also available.

Pinto Beans
Full-flavored, mealy-textured beans with distinctively mottled brown-and-tan skins. Similarly patterned cranberry beans may be substituted.

Red Beans
Oval beans, smaller and somewhat darker than kidney beans, with a similar texture and somewhat sweeter taste.

White (Navy) Beans
Small, white, thin-skinned, oval beans. Also known as Boston beans. Great Northern beans may be substituted.

BREAD CRUMBS
Fresh or dried bread crumbs are sometimes used to thicken puréed soups; browned in butter, they may also serve as a soup garnish. To make bread crumbs, choose a good-quality, rustic-style loaf made of unbleached wheat flour, with a firm, coarse-textured crumb; usually sold in bakeries as country-style, rustic or peasant bread. For fresh crumbs, cut away the crusts from the fresh bread and crumble the bread by hand or in a blender or a food processor fitted with the metal blade. For dried crumbs, crumble the bread as directed above, then spread the crumbs on a baking pan. Dry slowly, about 1 hour, in an oven set at its lowest temperature. Fine dried bread crumbs are also sold prepackaged.

CABBAGE, SAVOY
Firm, round, fine-flavored variety of cabbage with dark green leaves marked by a fine lacy pattern of veins.

CHERVIL
Herb with small leaves resembling flat-leaf (Italian) **parsley** and with a subtle flavor reminiscent of both parsley and anise. Used fresh to flavor delicate-tasting soups.

CHICKEN, STEWING
A mature chicken weighing 3–5 pounds (1.5–2.5 kg) or more, with highly flavorful flesh that is tougher than that of younger birds. Well-suited to making slowly simmered stock.

CHICKEN FAT, RENDERED

Commercial form of chicken fat rendered free of its connective tissue, leaving a thick, liquid fat with a rich chicken flavor. Popular in traditional Jewish cooking, it is available in ethnic delicatessens and some well-stocked food markets. Also known by the Yiddish term *schmaltz*.

CHILI OIL

Popular seasoning of sesame or vegetable oil in which hot **chilies** have been steeped. Available in Asian food shops and the specialty-food section of most supermarkets.

CLAMS

Bivalve mollusks prized for their sweet, tender flesh. Sold live in their shells, or sometimes already shucked, in good-quality fish markets or the seafood department of a food market. Discard any clams that do not close tightly upon touching. Once cooked, discard any clams that did not open.

For soup recipes that call for clams to be steamed open, first soak them for several minutes in enough cold water to cover generously. Under cold running water, scrub the shells clean with a small, stiff-bristled brush.

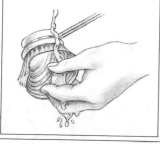

CHILIES

Any of a wide variety of peppers prized for the mild-to-hot spiciness they impart as a seasoning. Red, ripe chilies are sold fresh and dried. Fresh green chilies include the mild-to-hot, dark green poblano; the long, mild Anaheim or New Mexican chili; and the small, fiery jalapeño (below).

CILANTRO

Green, leafy herb resembling flat-leaf (Italian) **parsley**, with a sharp, aromatic, somewhat astringent flavor. Popular in Latin American and Asian soups. Also called fresh coriander and commonly referred to as Chinese parsley.

CRAB MEAT

Already-cooked crab meat is widely available in fish markets or the seafood counters of quality food markets. Most often, it has been frozen; for best flavor and texture, seek out fresh crab meat. When fresh crab is in season (September–April), fish markets will usually sell crabs boiled or steamed whole; ask for them to be cracked, so that you can open the shells by hand and remove the meat. Left in coarse chunks, the shelled meat, particularly from the body of the crab, is known and sold as "lump" crab meat; finer particles of crab meat, from the legs or broken down from larger lumps, is known as "flaked" crab meat. Avoid imitation crab meat (*surimi*).

CREAM

The terms *light* and *heavy* describe cream's butterfat content and related richness. Light cream, not available everywhere under this name, has a butterfat level varying from 18–30 percent. It is sometimes called coffee cream or table cream. If unavailable substitute equal parts heavy cream and half-and-half. Heavy cream has a butterfat content of at least 36 percent. For the best flavor and cooking properties, purchase fresh cream, avoiding long-lasting varieties that have been processed by ultraheat methods. In Britain, light cream is also known as single cream; use double cream for heavy cream.

CUMIN

Middle Eastern spice with a strong, dusky, aromatic flavor, popular in cuisines of its region of origin along with those of Latin America, India and parts of Europe. Sold either ground or as whole, small, crescent-shaped seeds

FISH SAUCE

Popular Southeast Asian seasoning prepared from salted, fermented fish, usually anchovies. Available in Asian food stores and food market specialty-food sections. Known variously as *nam pla* (Thai), *nuoc mam* (Vietnamese) and *patis* (Filipino).

GINGER

The rhizome of the tropical ginger plant, which yields a sweet, strong-flavored spice. Whole ginger rhizomes, commonly mistaken for roots, may be purchased fresh in a good-quality food market or well-stocked vegetable market. Ground dried ginger is easily found in jars or tins in any food market spice section.

HOT-PEPPER SAUCE

Bottled commercial cooking and table sauce made from fresh or dried hot red **chilies**. Many varieties are available, but Tabasco is the best-known brand.

KIRSCH

Dry, clear brandy distilled from black morello cherries and infused with their unique aroma and taste. Do not confuse with crème de kirsch, a sweet cherry liqueur.

LEEK

Sweet, moderately flavored member of the **onion** family, long and cylindrical in shape with a pale white root end and dark green leaves. Select firm, unblemished leeks, small to medium in size.

Grown in sandy soil, the leafy-topped, multilayered vegetables require thorough cleaning: First trim off the roots and the tough ends of the dark green leaves. If a recipe calls for leek whites only, trim off the dark green leaves where they meet the slender pale green part of the stem. Starting about 1 inch (2.5 cm) from the root end, slit the leek lengthwise. Vigorously swish the leek in a basin or sink filled with cold water. Drain and rinse again; check to make sure that no dirt remains between the tightly packed pale portion of the leaves.

LEMONGRASS

Thick, stalklike grass with a sharp, lemony flavor, popular in Southeast Asian cooking and available fresh or dried in Asian shops. If fresh lemongrass is unavailable, substitute 1 table-spoon dried lemongrass for each 8-inch (20-cm) stalk of fresh; or substitute long, thin strips of lemon peel.

LILY BUDS
The dried, unopened buds of tiger lilies (below), popular in Chinese cuisine for their subtle flavor, slightly chewy texture, delicate shape and pale tan color. Sometimes known by their translated Chinese name, golden needles. Available in Asian food stores.

LIME LEAVES
Small leaves of the lime tree, sold dried in Asian food shops and used as a subtle, citrusy seasoning in soups.

MATZO MEAL
A fine-textured meal ground from matzo, Jewish unleavened bread, and used as the main ingredient in matzo balls as well as in baking, as a breading for fried foods and as a thickening agent.

MIRIN
Sweetened Japanese rice wine used as a flavoring ingredient. Medium-dry sherry may be substituted.

MISO PASTE
A thick, rich-tasting paste fermented from cooked soybeans, wheat or rice, and salt, used as a seasoning in Japanese cooking. The two most common forms are the more robust red miso (*aka miso*) and the milder white miso (*shiro miso*). Available in Japanese food shops and some well-stocked food markets.

MUNG BEAN SPROUTS
The most commonly available form of bean sprouts found in well-stocked food markets and vegetable markets. Mild-tasting, crisp, pale in color and 2–3 inches (5–7.5 cm) in length.

MUSHROOMS, PORCINI
Widely used Italian term for *Boletus edulis,* a popular wild mushroom with a rich, meaty flavor. Most commonly sold in dried form (below) in Italian delicatessens and specialty-food shops, to be reconstituted in liquid as a flavoring for soups, stews, sauces and stuffings. Also known by the French term *cèpe.*

MUSHROOMS, SHIITAKE
Meaty-flavored Asian mushroom variety with flat, dark brown caps usually 2–3 inches (5–7.5 cm) in diameter. Available fresh in well-stocked greengrocers and food markets; also sold dried, to be soaked in warm water to cover to soften for approximately 20 minutes before use.

MUSHROOMS, STRAW
Small, plump, brown mushrooms resembling closed umbrellas, named for the beds of straw on which they grow in China. The canned variety, most often used, is available in Asian food stores.

OIL, OLIVE
When a soup recipe calls for olive oil, extra-virgin olive oil, extracted from olives on the first pressing without use of heat or chemicals, is preferred—particularly in the cold Spanish soup known as gazpacho, which gets some of its characteristic flavor and texture from the oil.

OIL, SESAME
Rich, flavorful and aromatic oil pressed from sesame seeds. Those from China and Japan, sometimes referred to as Asian sesame oil, are made from roasted sesame seeds, resulting in a darker, stronger oil used as a flavoring ingredient; its low smoking temperature and intense flavor make Asian sesame oil unsuitable for using alone for cooking.

OKRA
Small, mild-flavored, slender green vegetable-fruit pods, about 1½–3 inches (4–7.5 cm) in length, with crisp outer flesh and thick, mucilaginous juices that add body to such soups as Creole gumbo.

ONION, GREEN
Variety of onion harvested immature, leaves and all, before its bulb has formed. Green and white parts may both be enjoyed, raw or cooked, for their mild but still pronounced onion flavor, particularly when used as a garnish. Also called spring onion or scallion.

ONION, RED
Mild, sweet variety of onion with purplish red skin and red-tinged white flesh. Also known as Spanish onion.

ONION, YELLOW
Common, white-fleshed, strong-flavored onion distinguished by its dry, yellowish brown skin.

ORZO
Small, rice-shaped form of pasta.

PAPRIKA
Powdered spice derived from the dried paprika pepper; popular in

PEPPER, BELL
Fresh, sweet-fleshed, bell-shaped member of the pepper family. Also known as capsicum. Most common in the unripe green form, although ripened red or yellow varieties are available as well. Creamy pale yellow, orange and purple-black types may also be found.

To prepare a raw bell pepper, cut it in half lengthwise with a sharp knife. Pull out the stem section from each half, along with the cluster of seeds attached to it. Remove any remaining seeds, along with any thin white membranes, or ribs, to which they are attached. Cut the pepper halves into quarters, strips or thin slices, as called for in the specific recipe.

When a recipe calls for roasted bell peppers, place the whole peppers on a baking sheet. Roast in a 400°F (200°C) oven, under a broiler (griller) or atop a grill, turning occasionally, until their skins are evenly blackened. Cover with a cotton towel and, as soon as they are cool enough to handle, peel off the blackened skins and remove the stems, seeds and ribs. Then cut the peppers as directed in the recipe.

several European cuisines and available in sweet, mild and hot forms. Hungarian paprika is the best, but Spanish paprika, which is mild, may also be used. Buy in small quantities from shops with a high turnover, to ensure a fresh, flavorful supply.

PARSLEY
This popular fresh herb is available in two varieties, the more popular curly-leaf type and a flat-leaf type. The latter, also known as Italian parsley, has a more pronounced flavor and is preferred.

PEARL BARLEY
Whole kernels of the mild-tasting grain that are polished four to six times during processing, resulting in a smooth surface and lustrous gray finish resembling a pearl. Available in most food markets and natural-food stores.

PEPPER
Pepper, the most common of all savory spices, is best purchased as whole peppercorns, to be ground in a pepper mill as needed, or coarsely crushed. Pungent black peppercorns derive from slightly underripe pepper berries, whose hulls oxidize as they dry. Milder white peppercorns come from fully ripened berries, with the husks removed before drying.

RAMEN
Yellow Japanese wheat noodles, sold fresh or dried and commonly used in soups or stir-fried dishes. Sold in Japanese food stores and most well-stocked food markets. Packaged instant *ramen*, which is more widely available, should not be used for recipes in this book.

RED PEPPER FLAKES
Coarsely ground flakes of dried red **chilies**, including seeds, which add moderately hot flavor to the foods they season.

SAFFRON
Intensely aromatic, golden orange spice made from the dried stigmas of a species of crocus; used to perfume and color many classic Mediterranean and East Indian dishes. Sold either as threads—the dried stigmas—or in powdered form. Look for products labeled "pure saffron."

SAUSAGE, ANDOUILLE
Creole-Cajun smoked pork sausage highly seasoned with red pepper and garlic. Sold in good-quality meat markets, specialty-food shops and better food markets.

SAUSAGE, CHORIZO
Mexican- or Spanish-style coarse-textured fresh pork sausage spiced with hot **chilies** and other seasonings. Available in Latin American food stores and meat markets and in better food markets.

SAVORY, SUMMER
Delicate green herb that complements the flavors of vegetables, seafood and poultry. Best in its fresh form, although also widely available dried.

SHALLOT
Small member of the onion family with brown skin, white-to-purple flesh and a flavor resembling a cross between sweet onion and garlic.

SHERRY
Fortified, cask-aged wine, ranging in varieties from dry to sweet. Enjoyed as an aperitif and used as a flavoring in both savory and sweet recipes.

SHRIMP
Raw shrimp (prawns) are usually sold with the heads already removed but the shells still intact. Before cooking, they are often peeled and their thin, veinlike intestinal tracts removed.

Using your thumbs, split open the shrimp's thin shell along the concave side, between its two rows of legs. Peel away the shell, taking care to leave the last segment with tail fin intact and attached to the meat.

With a small, sharp knife, carefully make a shallow slit along the peeled shrimp's back, just deep enough to expose the long, usually dark, veinlike intestinal tract. With the tip of the knife or your fingers, lift up and pull out the vein, discarding it.

TOMATOES
During summer, when tomatoes are in season, use the best sun-ripened tomatoes you can find. At other times of year, plum tomatoes, sometimes called Roma or egg tomatoes, are likely to have the best flavor and texture. To peel fresh tomatoes, first bring a saucepan of water to a boil. Using a small, sharp knife, cut out the core from the stem end of the tomato. Then cut a shallow X in the skin at the tomato's base. Submerge for about 20 seconds in the boiling water, then remove and dip in a bowl of cold water. Starting at the X, peel the skin from the tomato, using your fingertips and, if necessary, the knife blade. Cut the tomatoes in half and turn each half cut-side down. Then cut as directed in individual recipes. To seed a tomato, cut it in half crosswise. Squeeze gently to force out the seed sacks.

VINEGARS
Literally "sour" wine, vinegar results when certain strains of yeast cause wine to ferment for a second time, turning it acidic. The best-quality wine vinegars begin with good-quality wine. Red wine vinegar, like the wine from which it is made, has a more robust flavor than vinegar produced from white wine. Balsamic vinegar, a specialty of Modena, Italy, is made from reduced grape juice and aged for many years. Vinegars are also made from other alcoholic liquids such as apple cider and Japanese rice wine.

ZEST
Thin, brightly colored, outermost layer of a citrus fruit's peel, containing most of its aromatic essential oils—a lively source of flavor.

Index

ACKNOWLEDGMENTS

The publishers would like to thank the following people and organizations for their generous assistance and support in producing this book: Sharon C. Lott, Stephen W. Griswold, Tara Brown, James Obata, Ken DellaPenta, the buyers for Gardener's Eden, and the buyers and store managers for Pottery Barn and Williams-Sonoma stores.

The following kindly lent props for the photography:
Biordi Art Imports, Fillamento, Stephanie Greenleigh, Sue Fisher King, Karen Nicks, Lorraine and Judson Puckett, Wendely Harvey, Sue White and Chuck Williams.